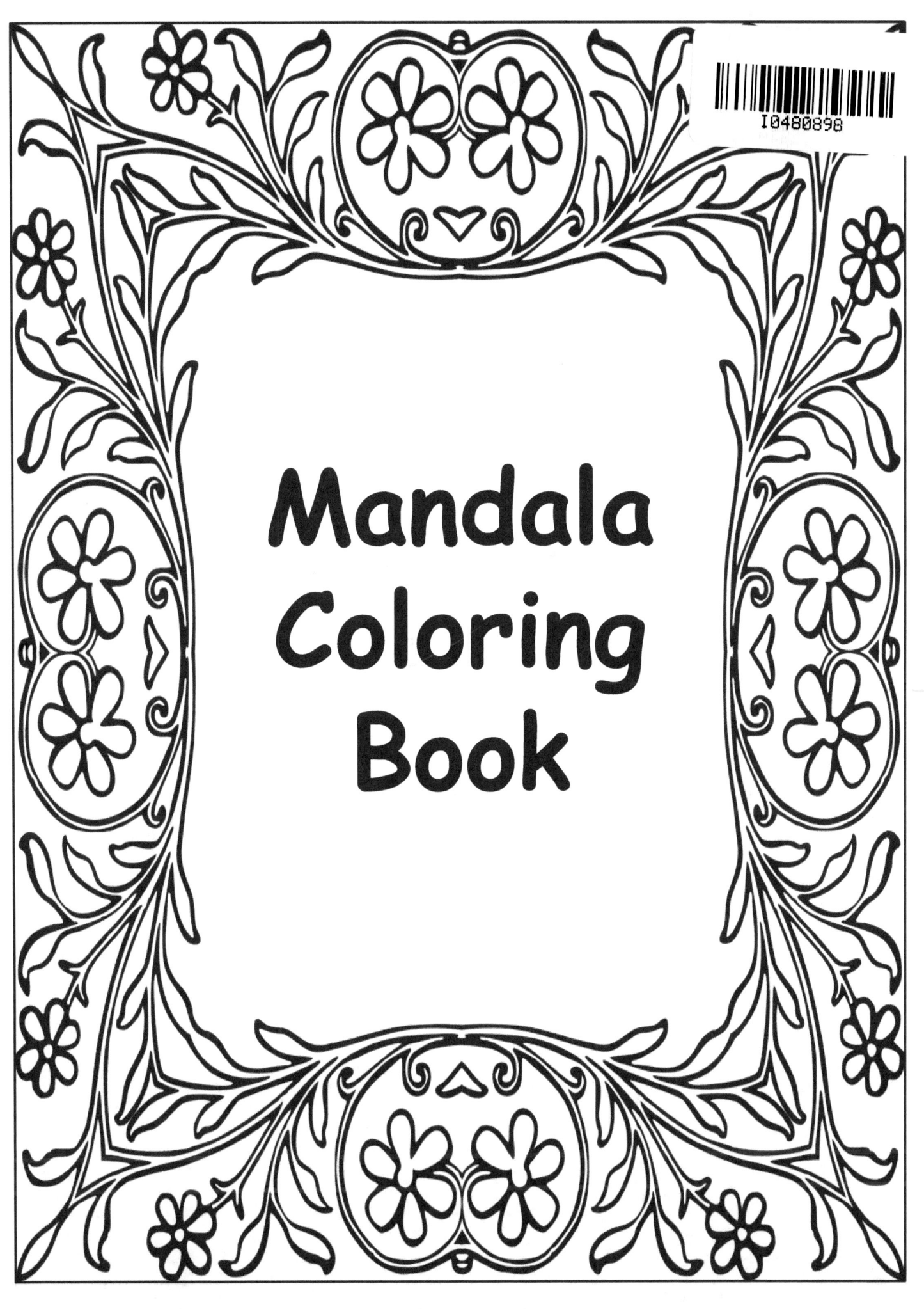

Mandala Coloring Book

Mandala Coloring Book For Adults Relaxation and stress relief.

There are About 50 single side mandalas in this book, and all are lovely. A lot of them have some finer details

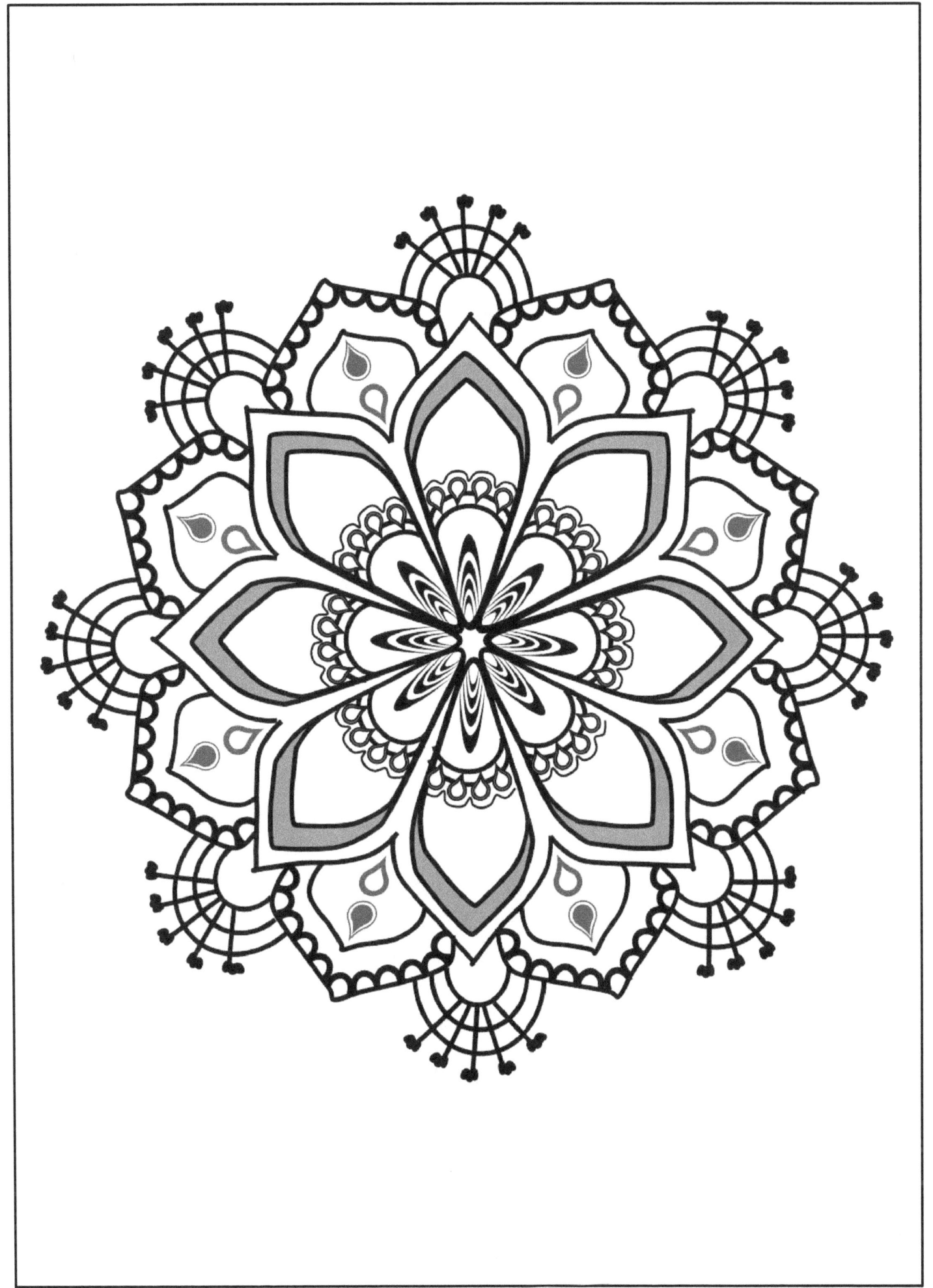

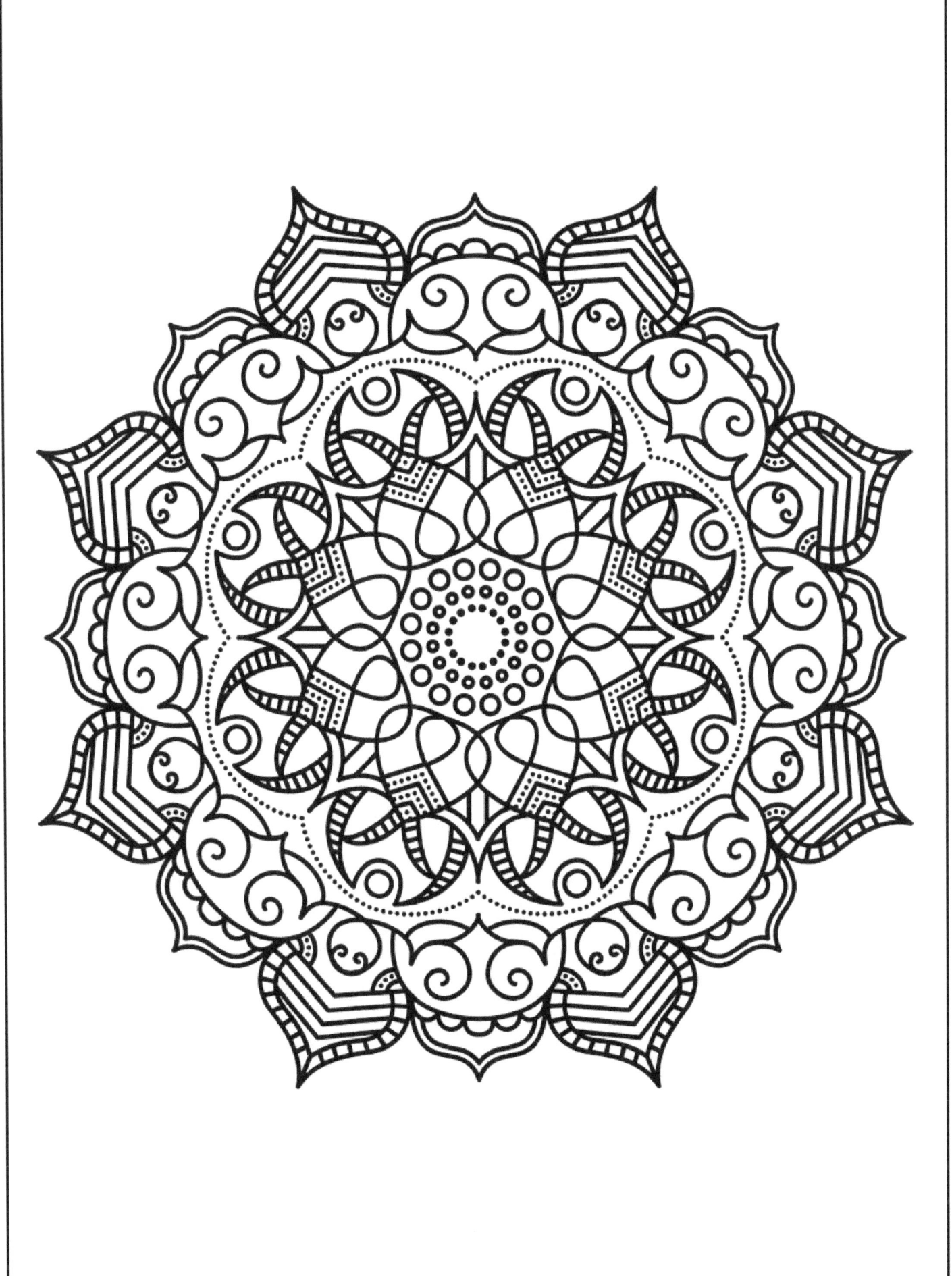

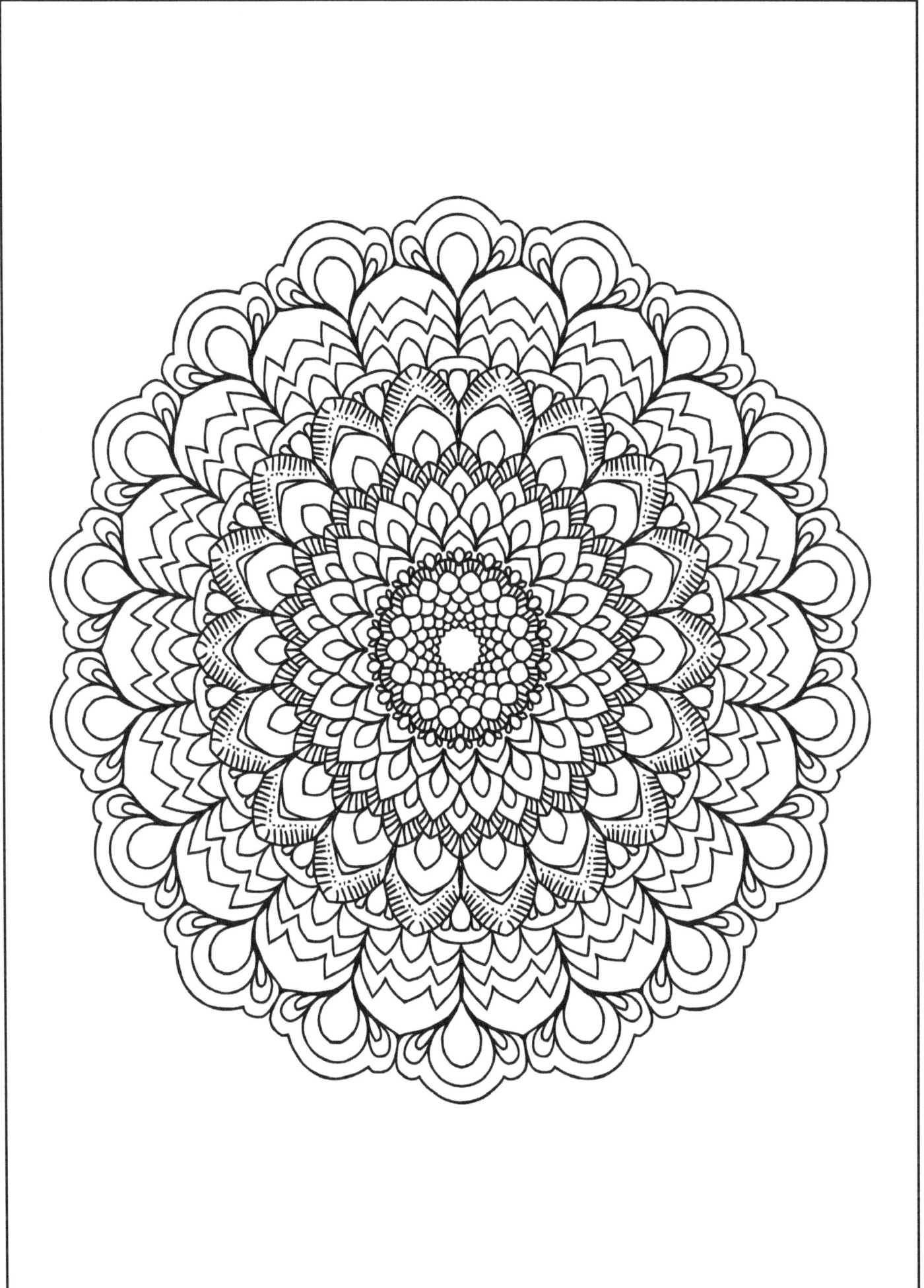

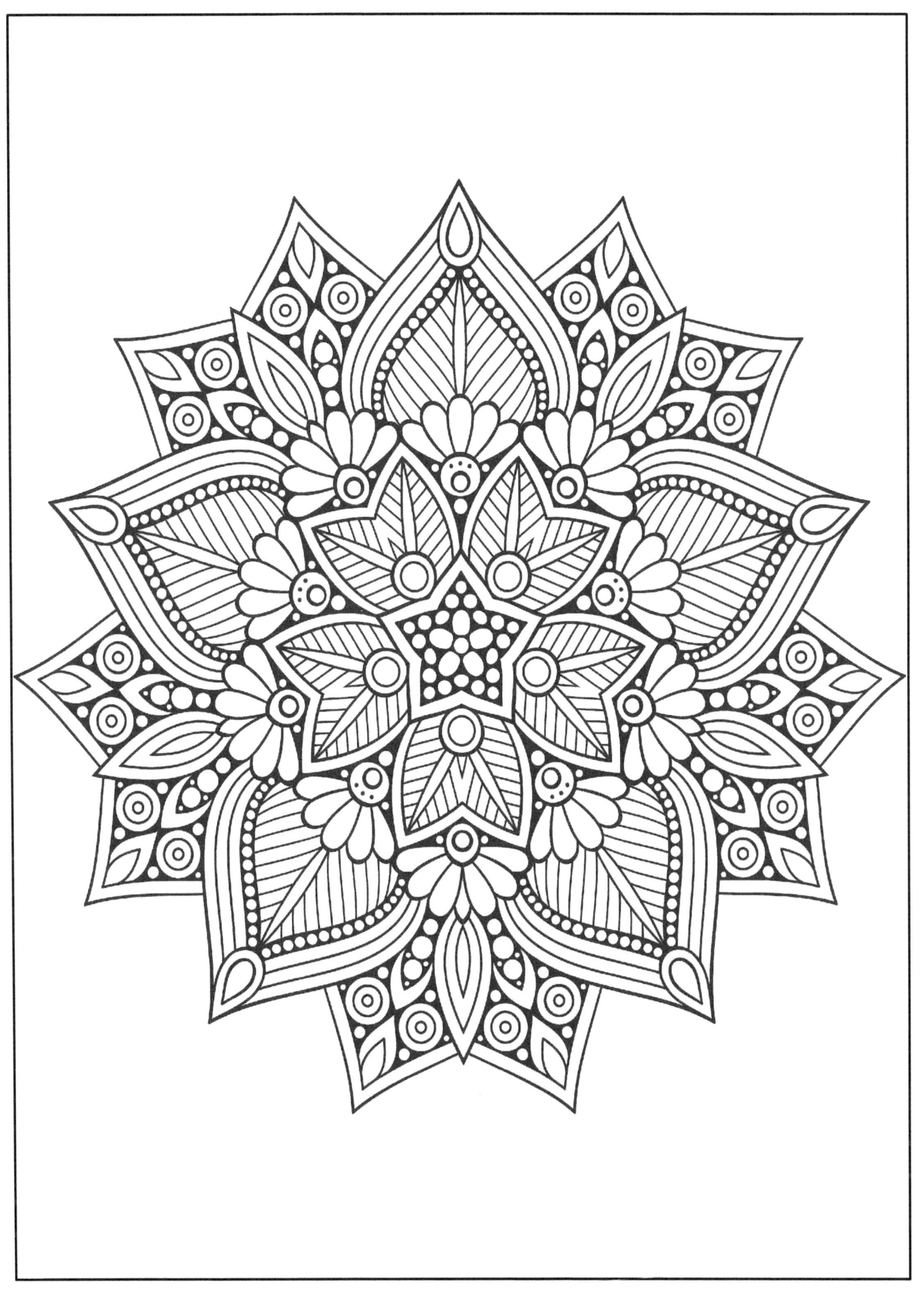

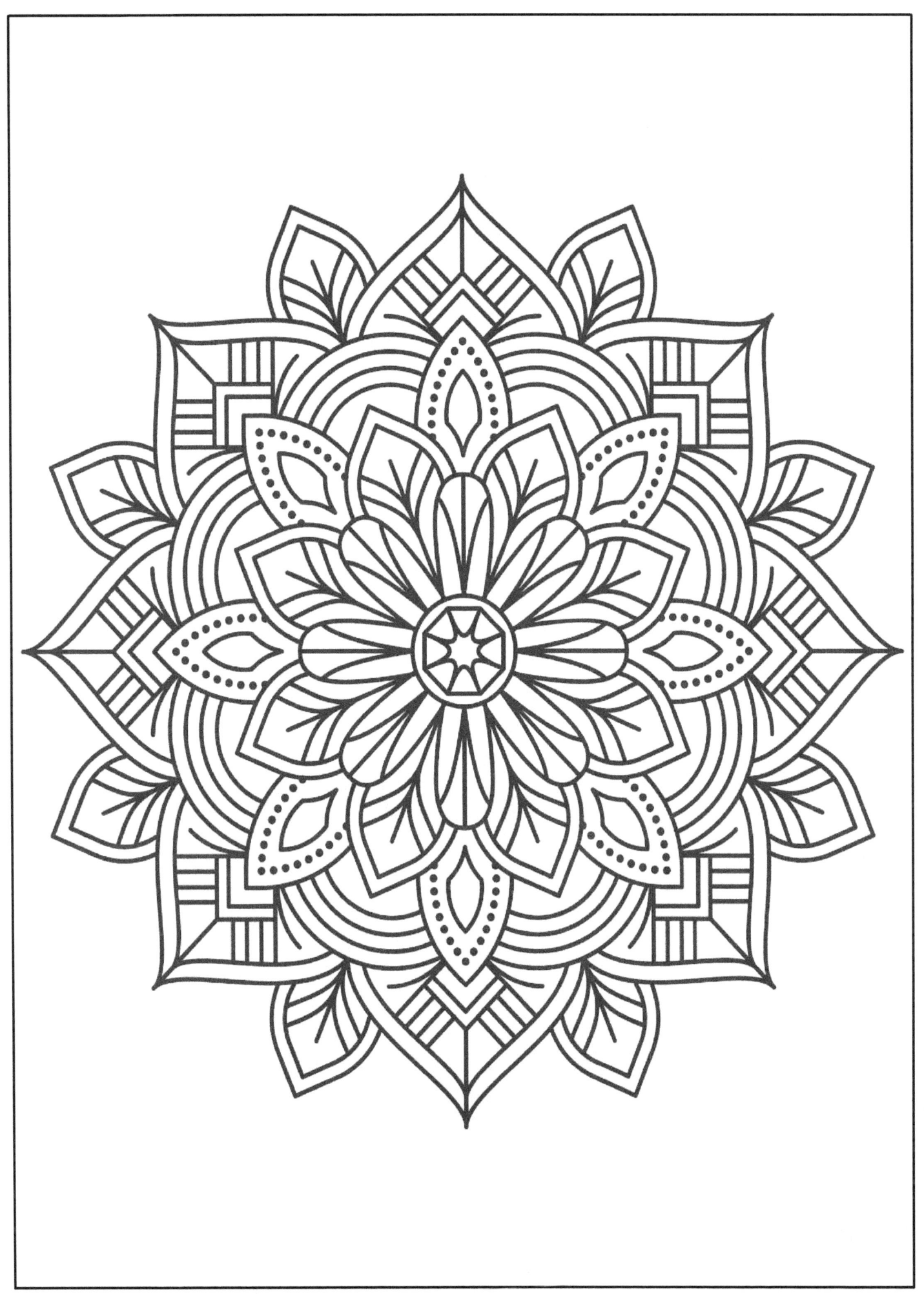

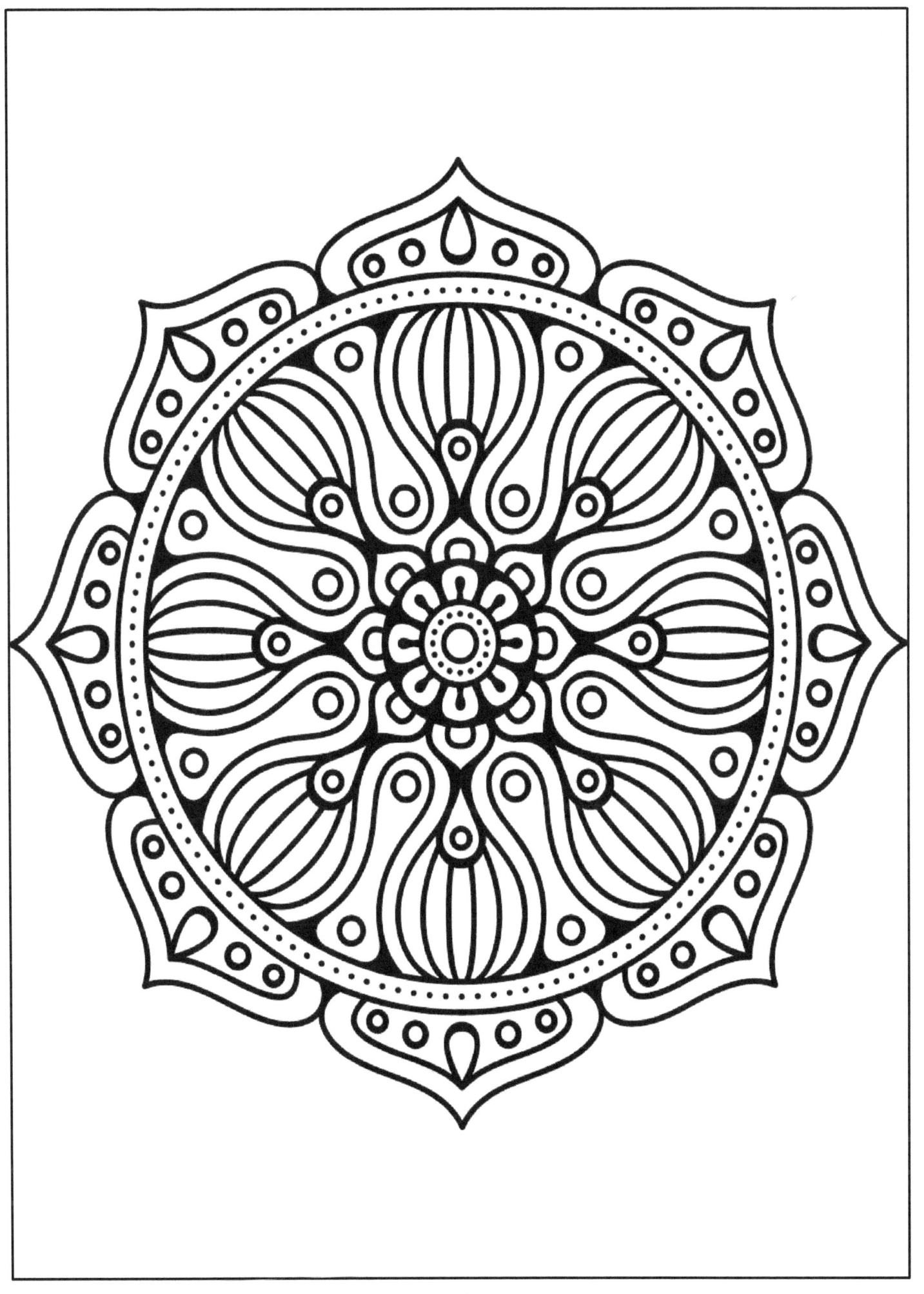

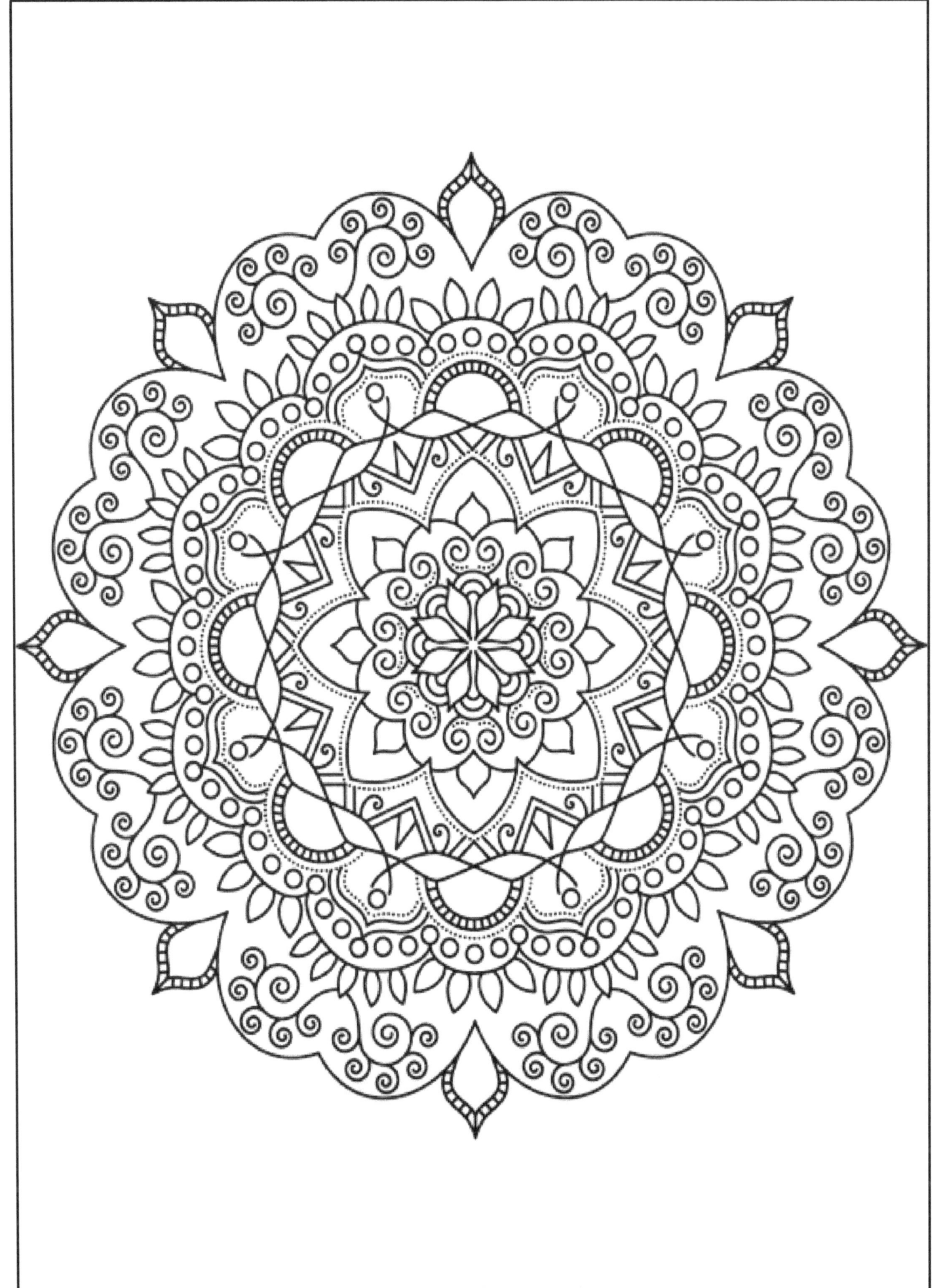

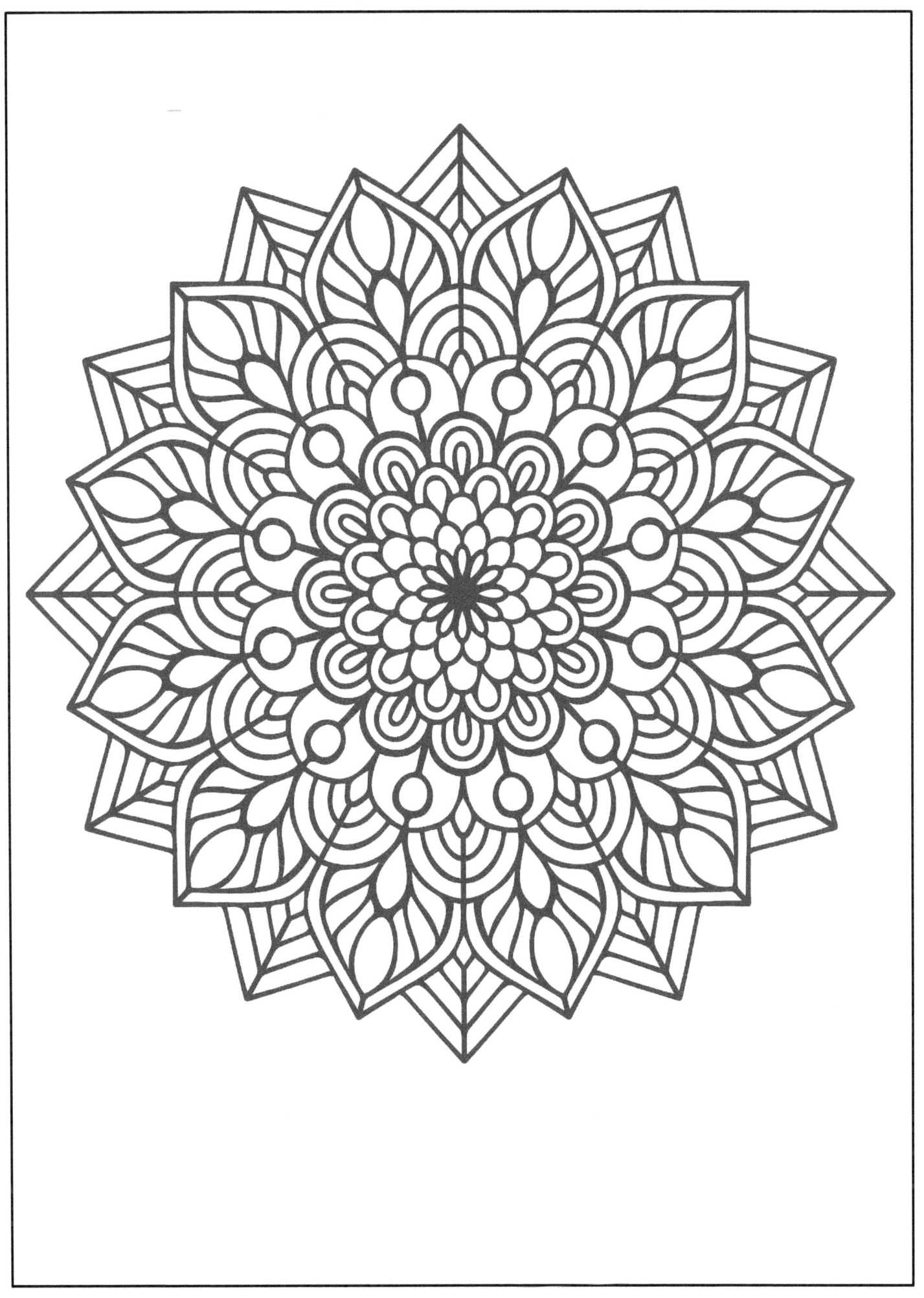

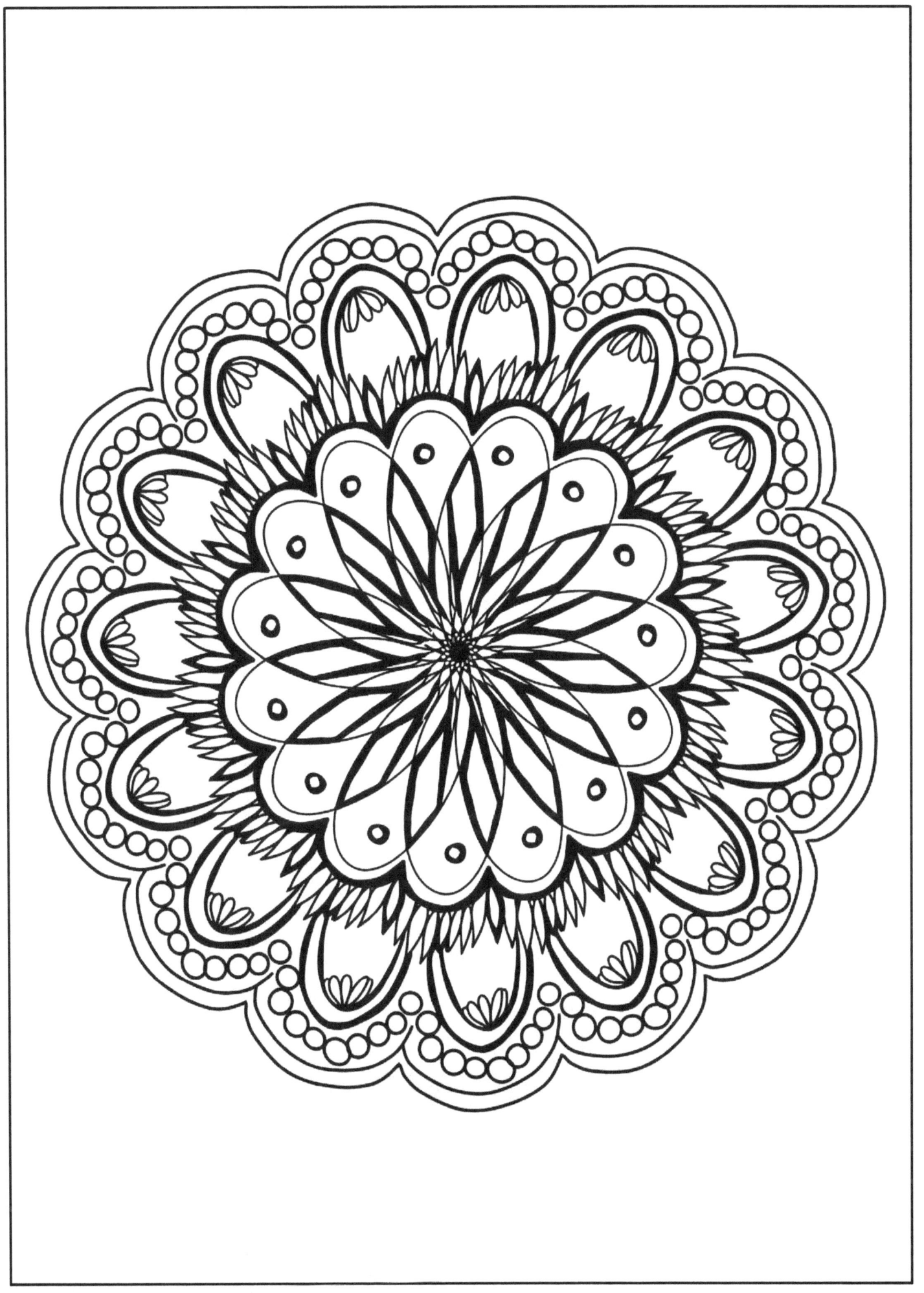

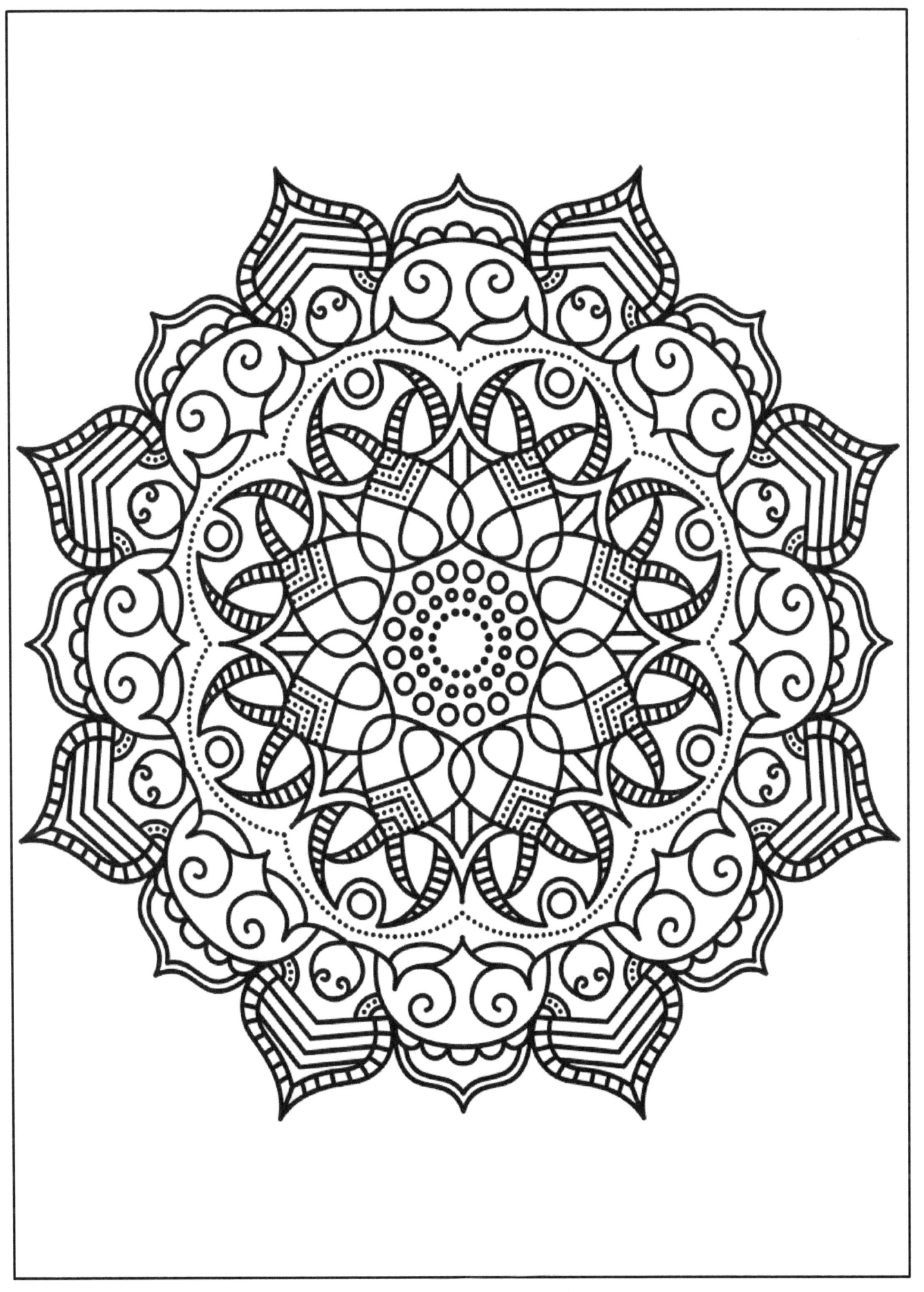

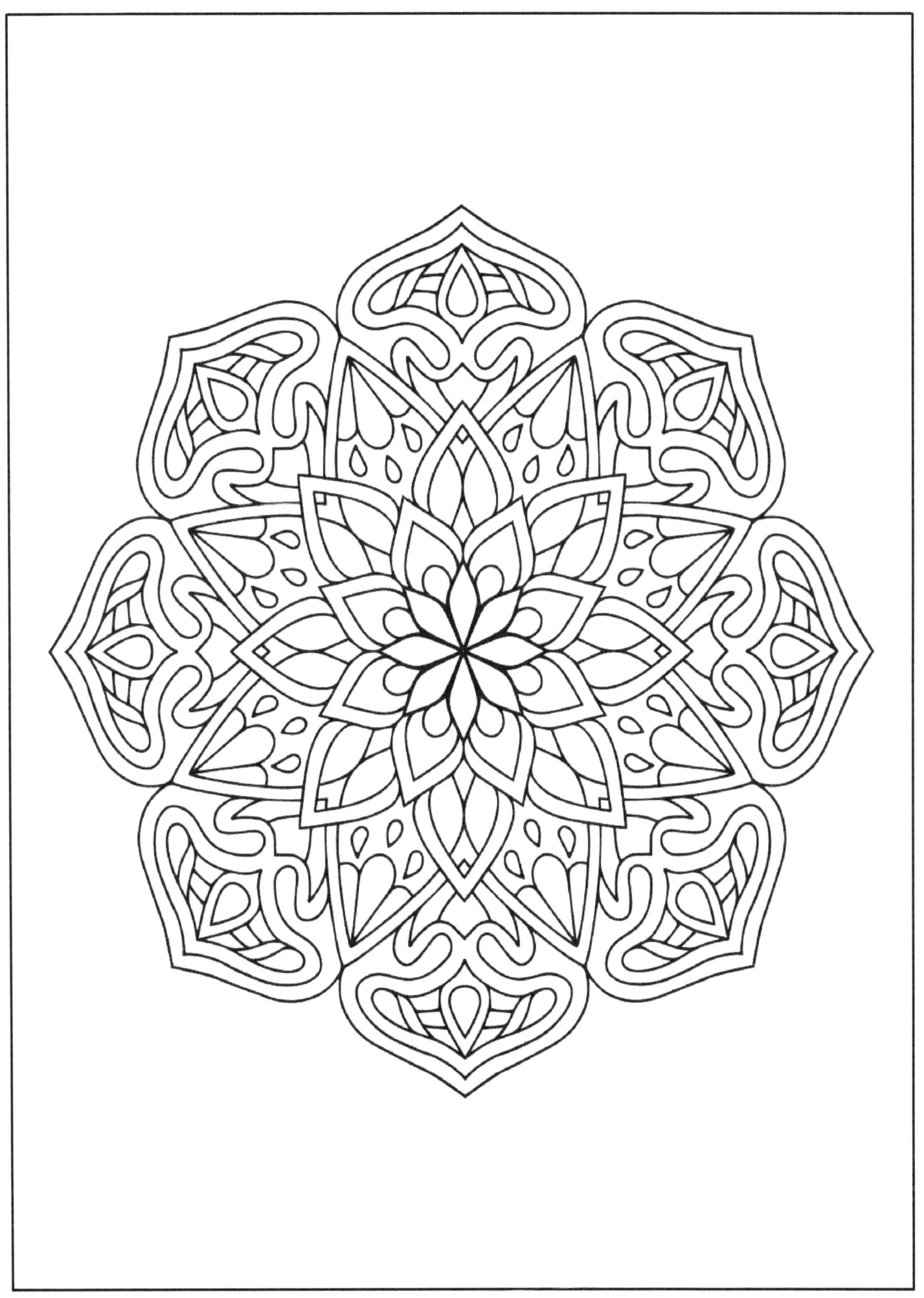

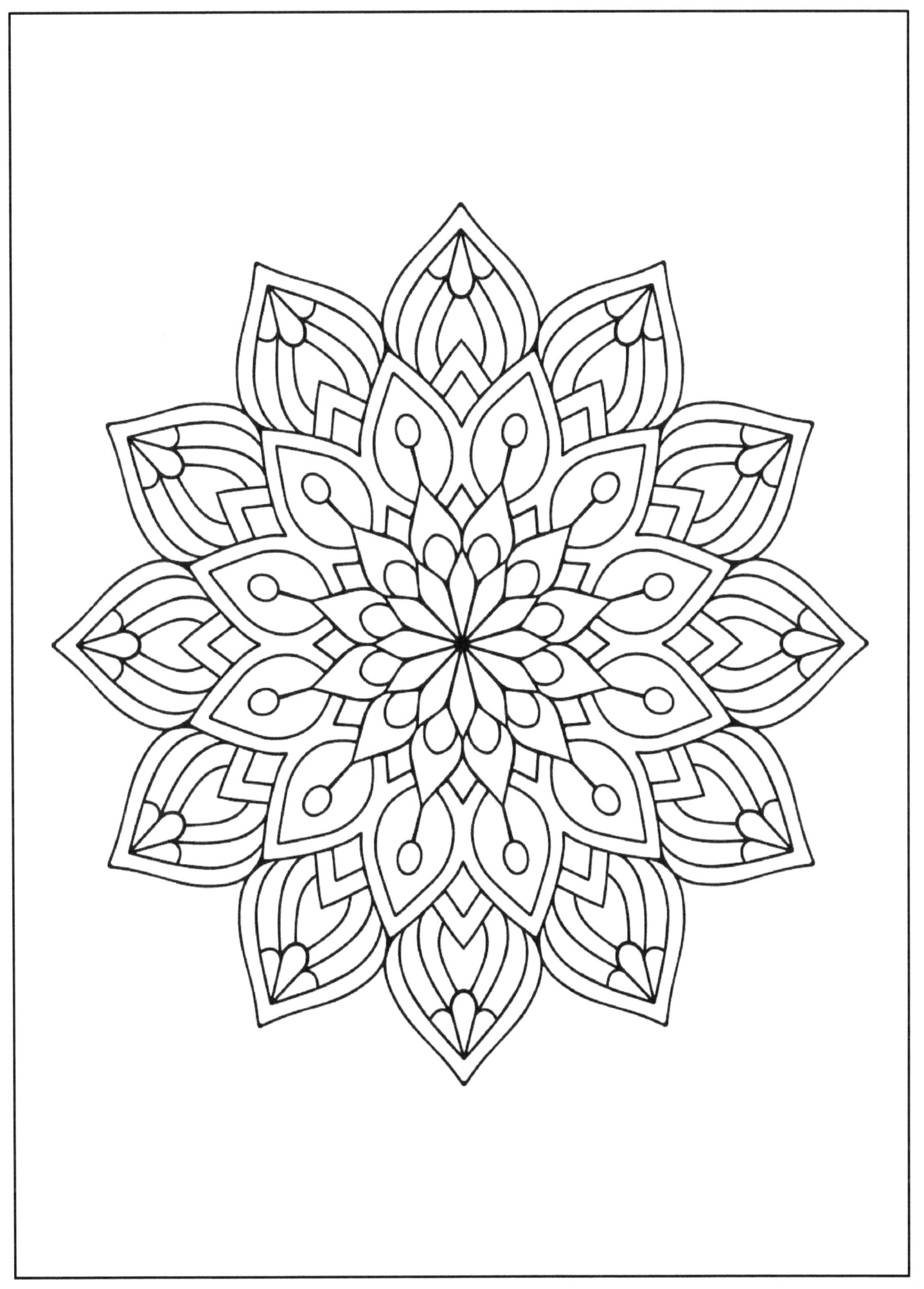

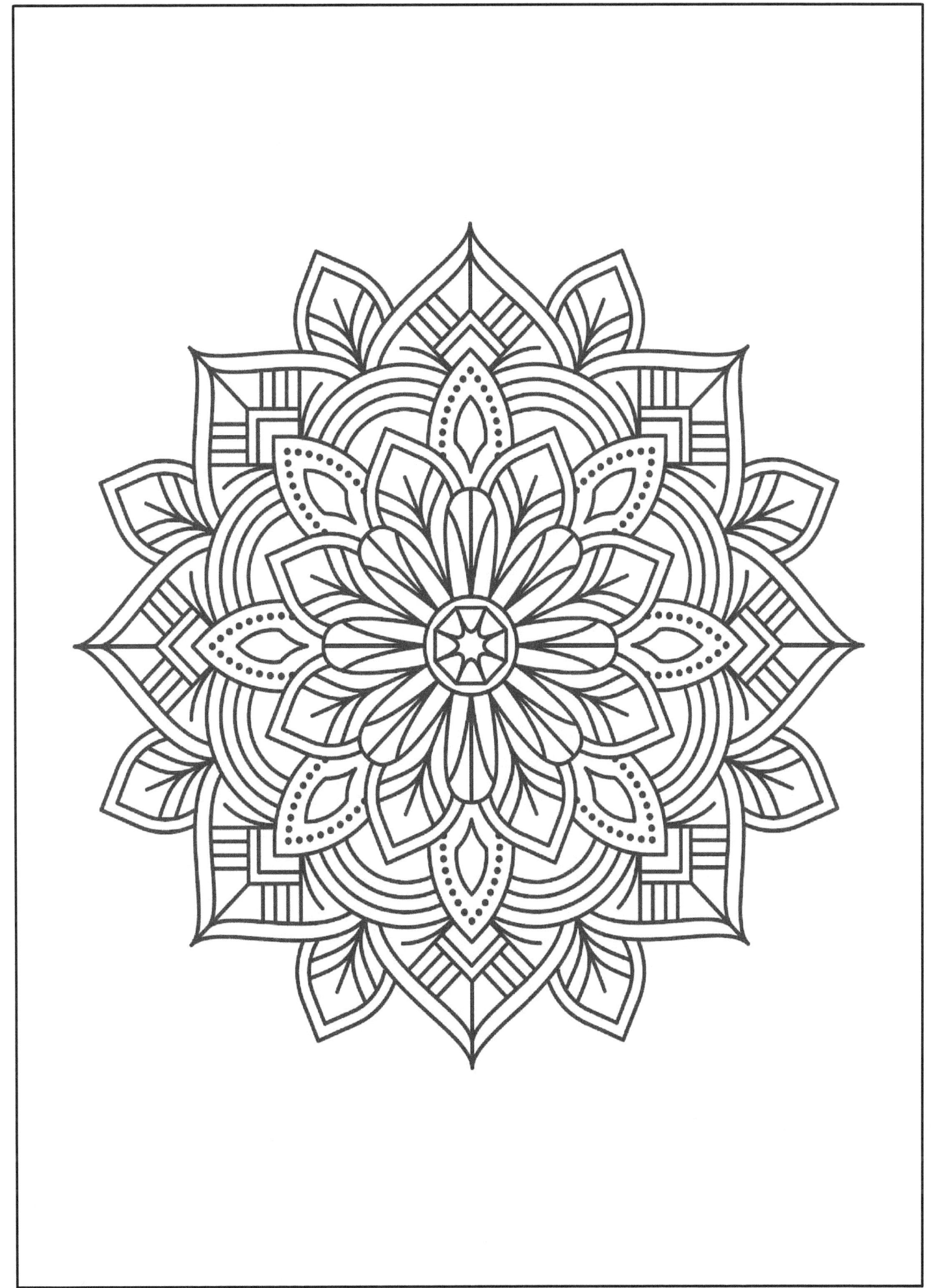

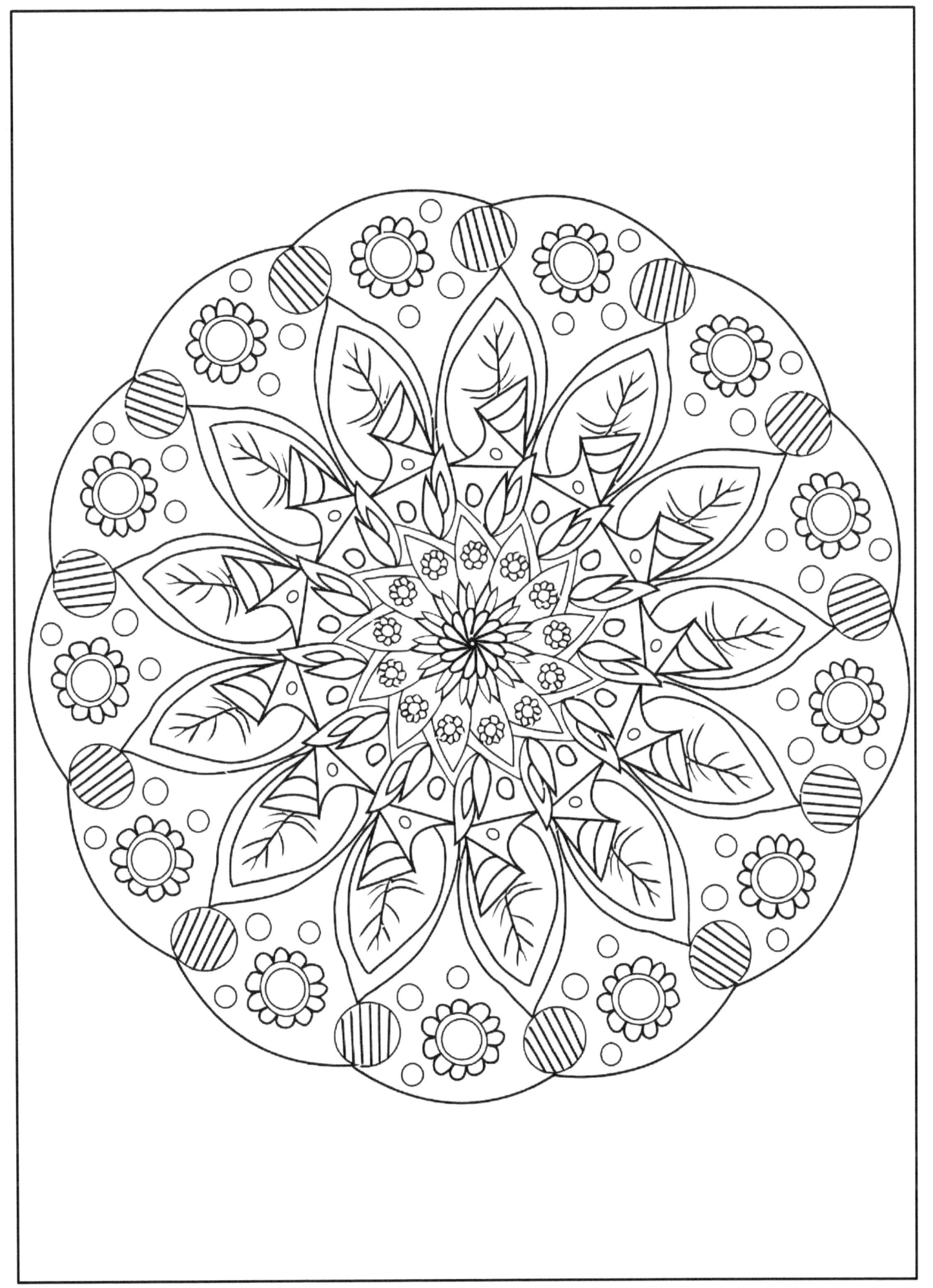

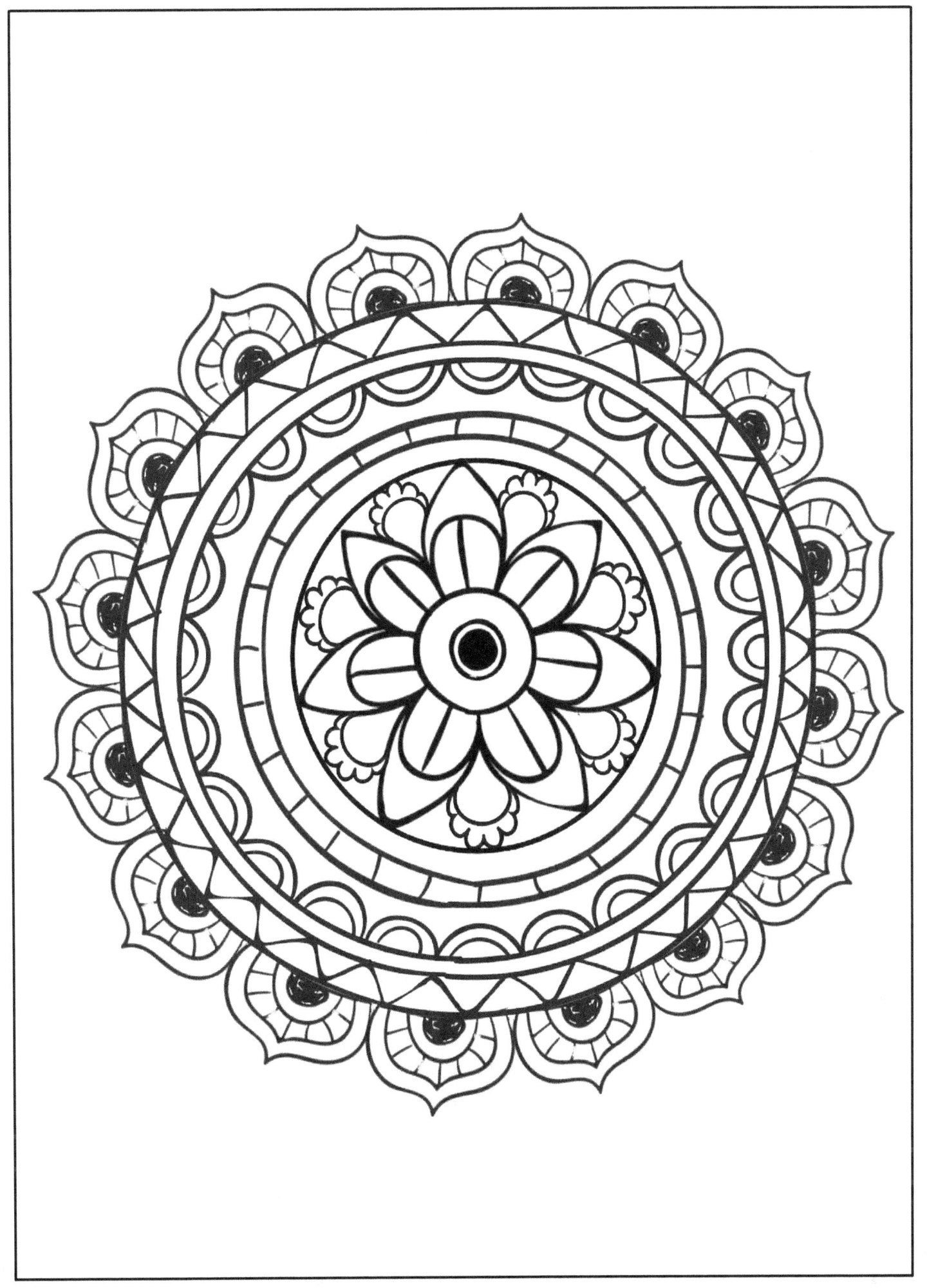

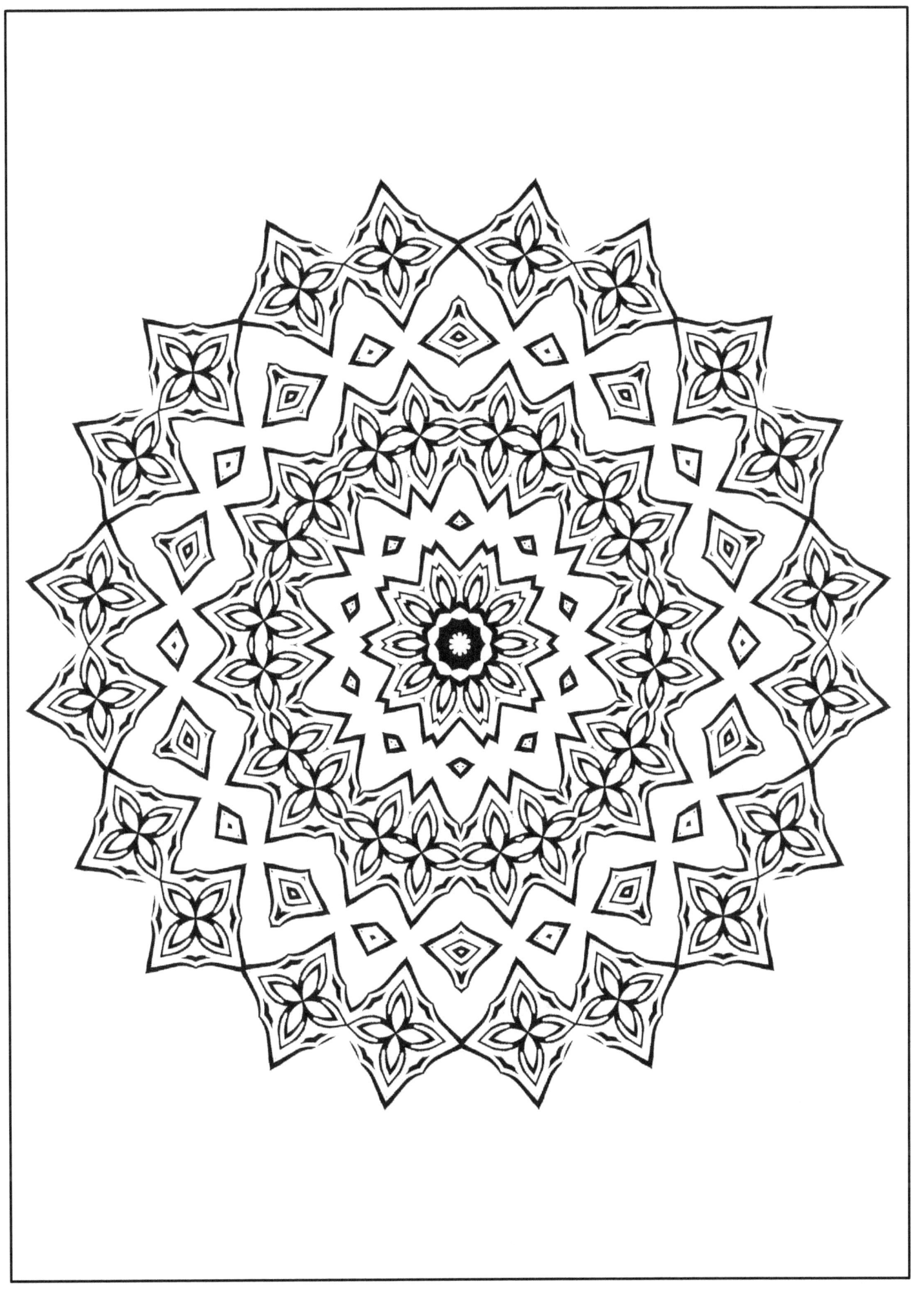

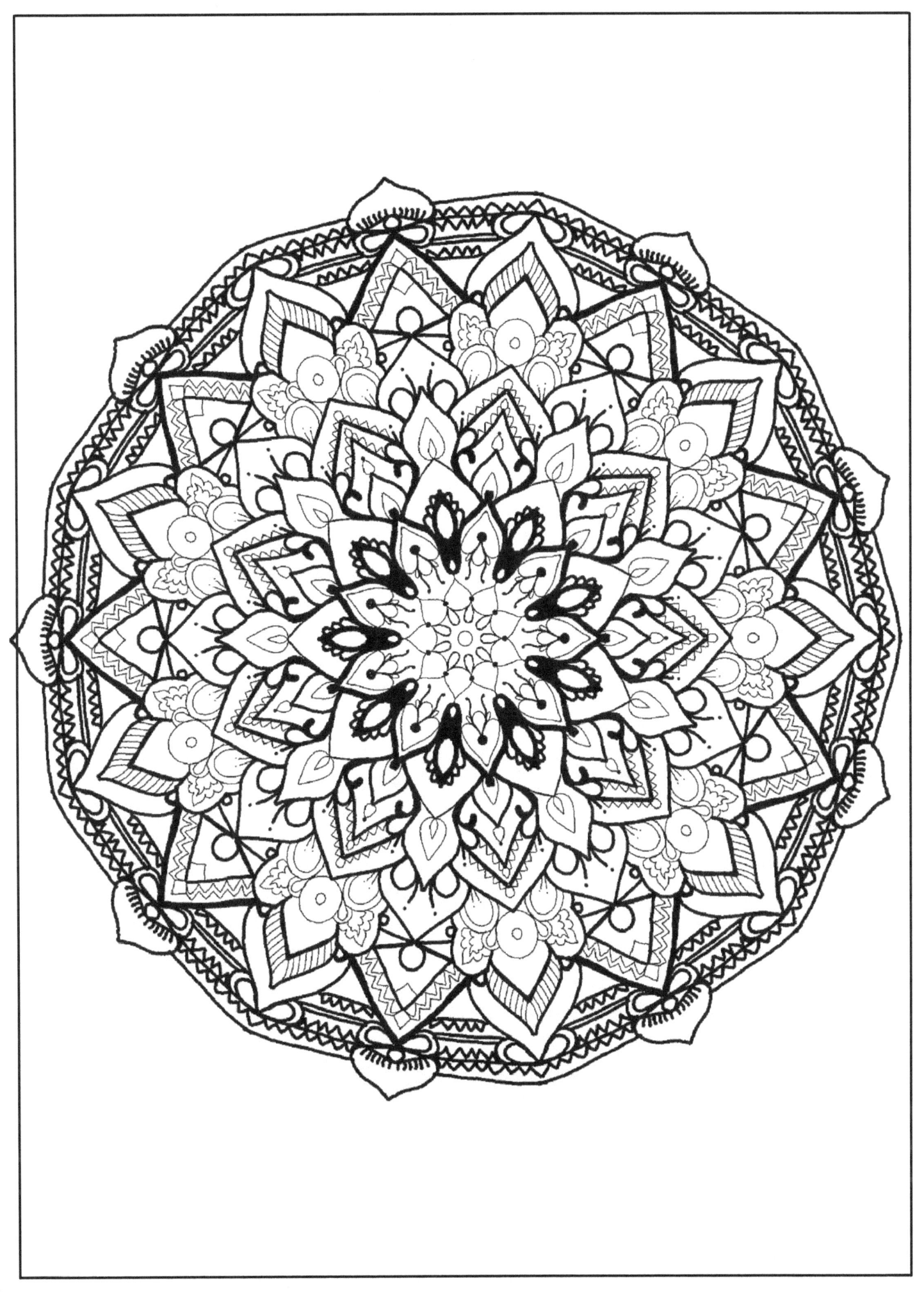

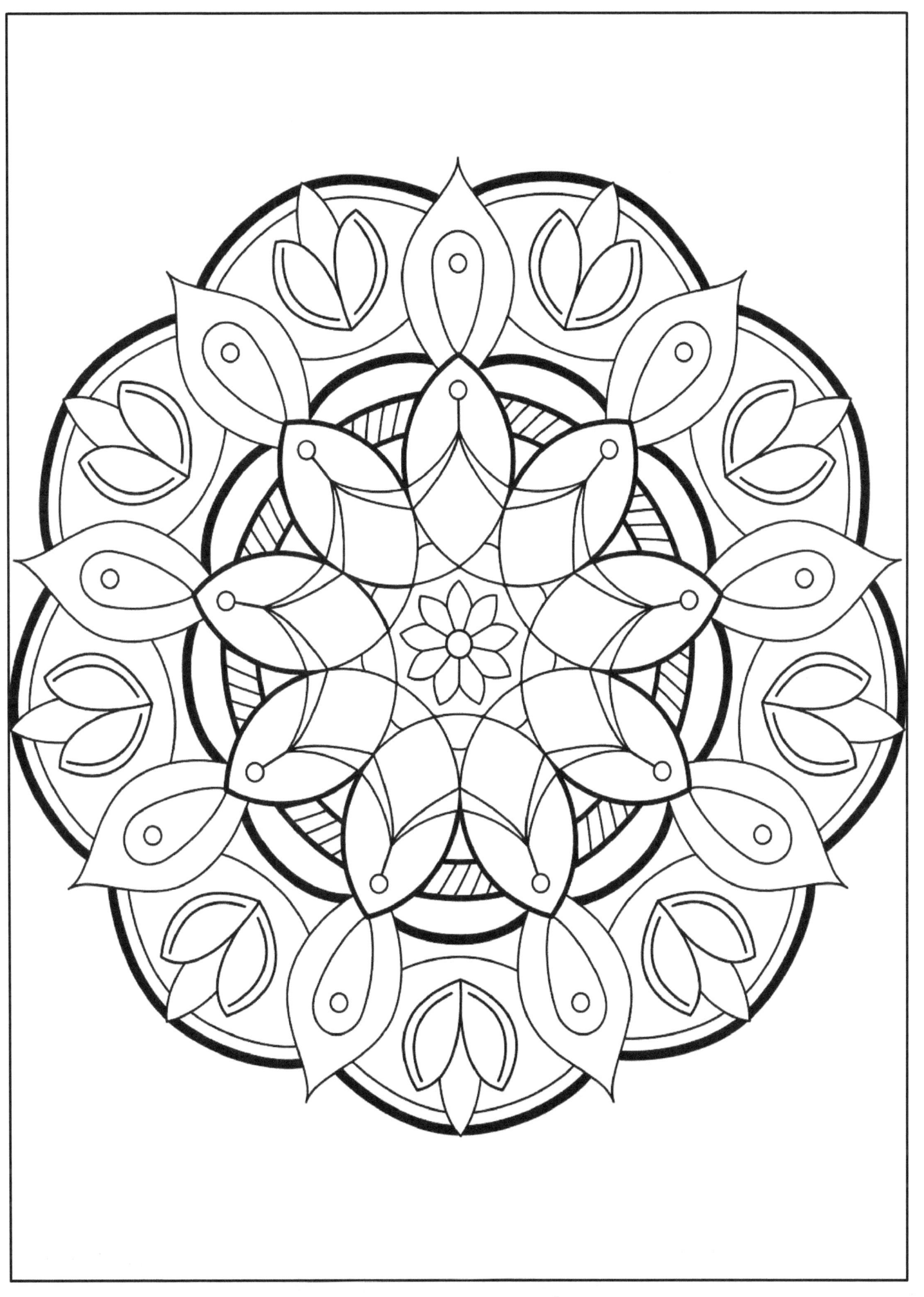

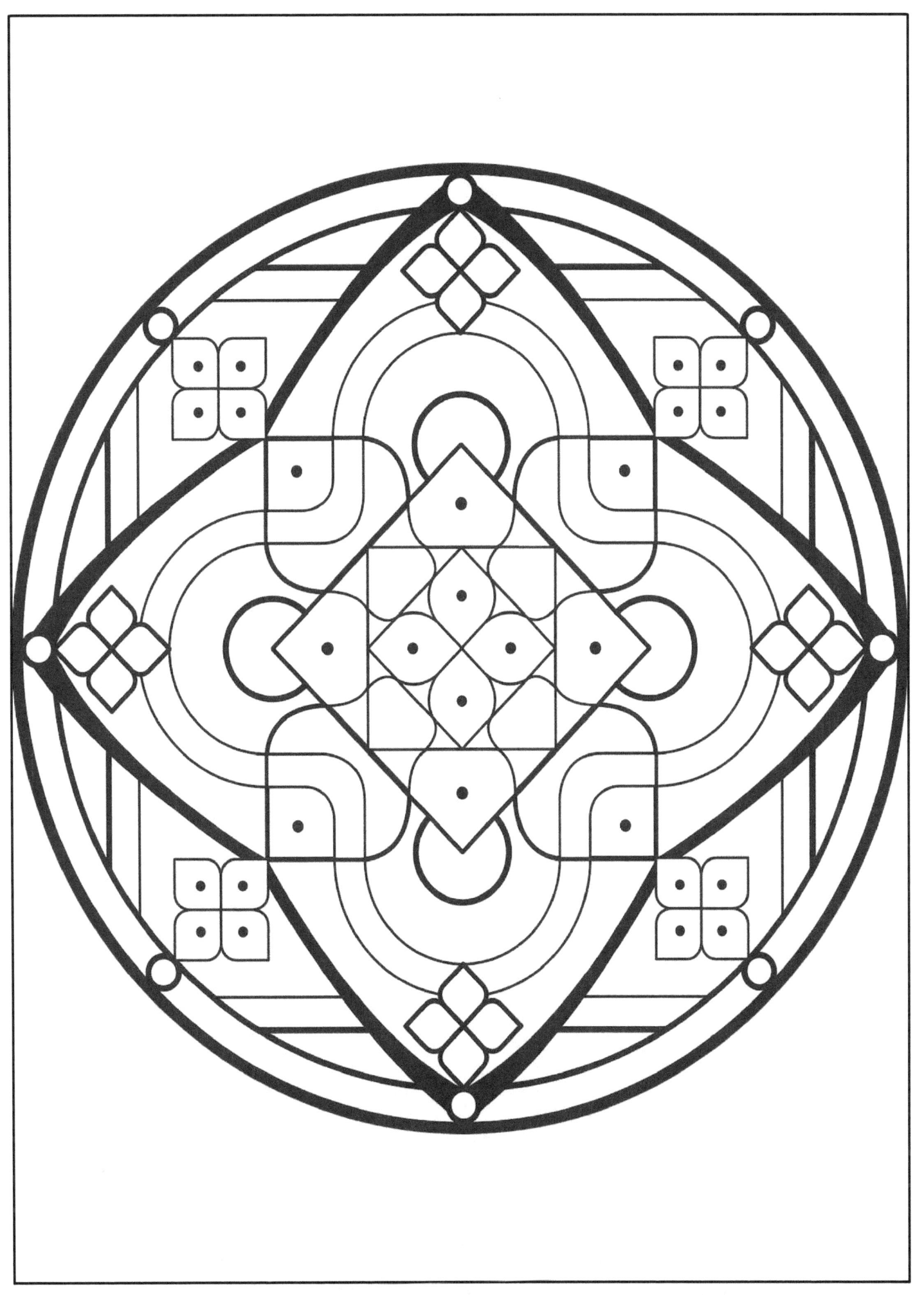

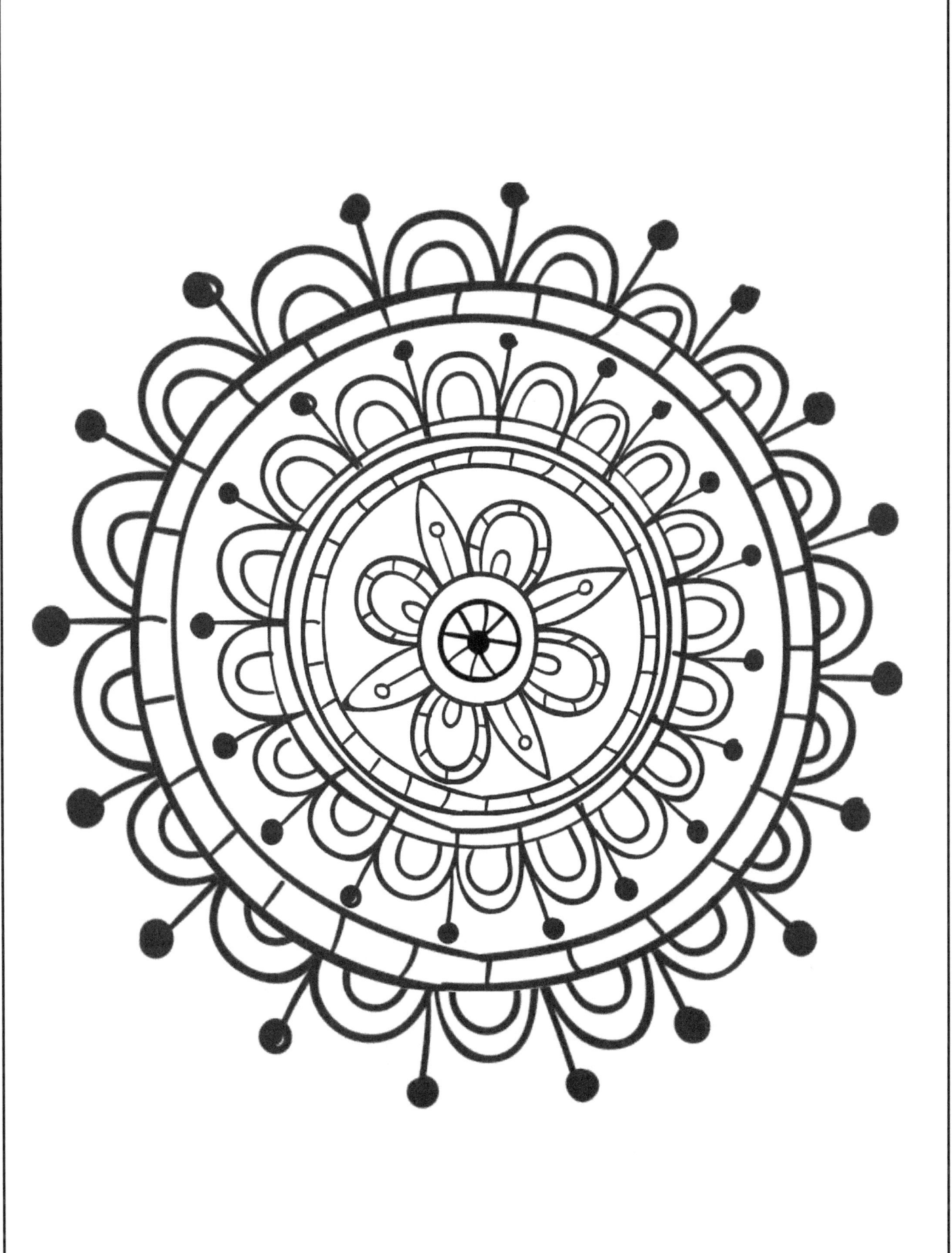

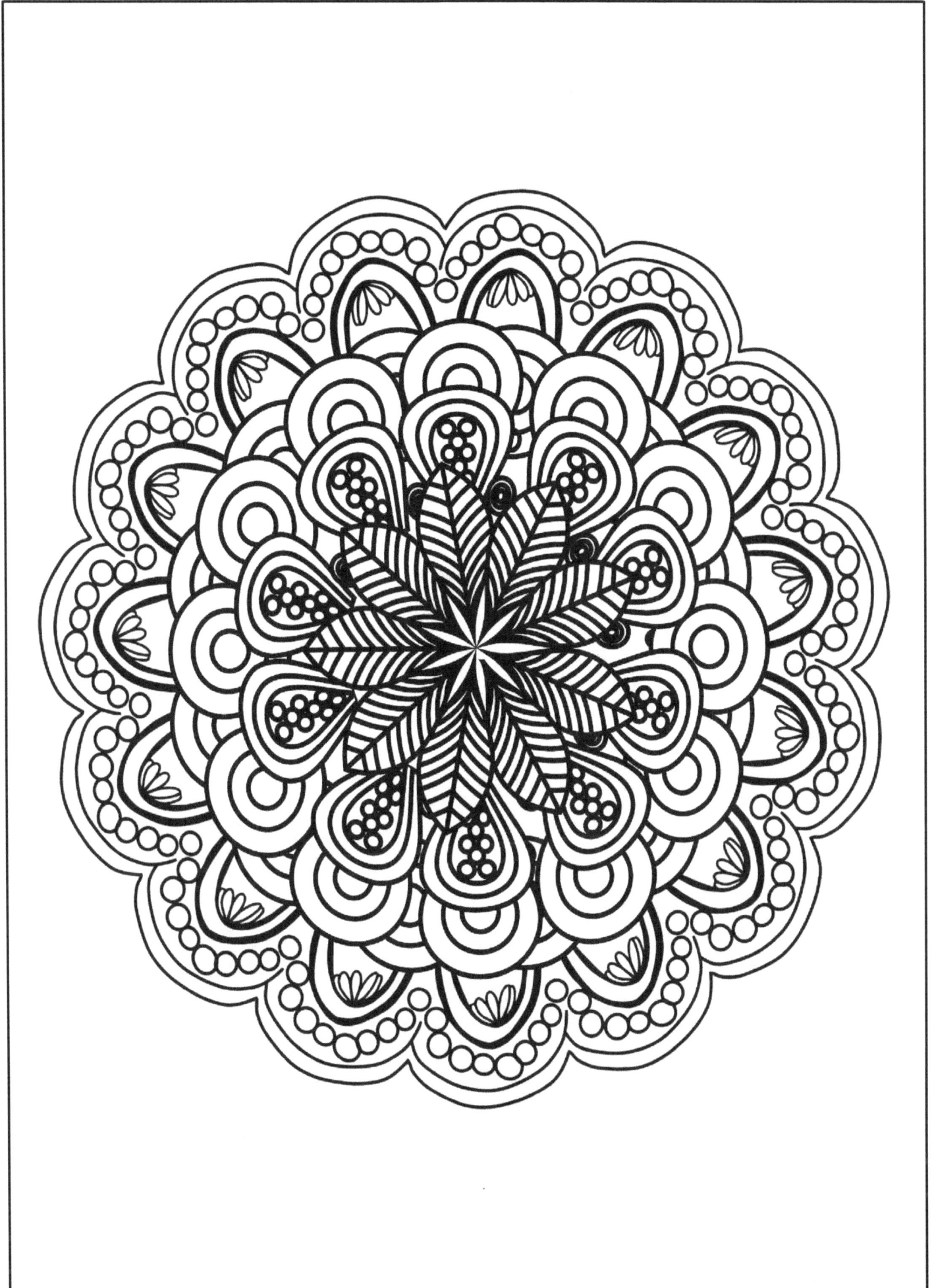

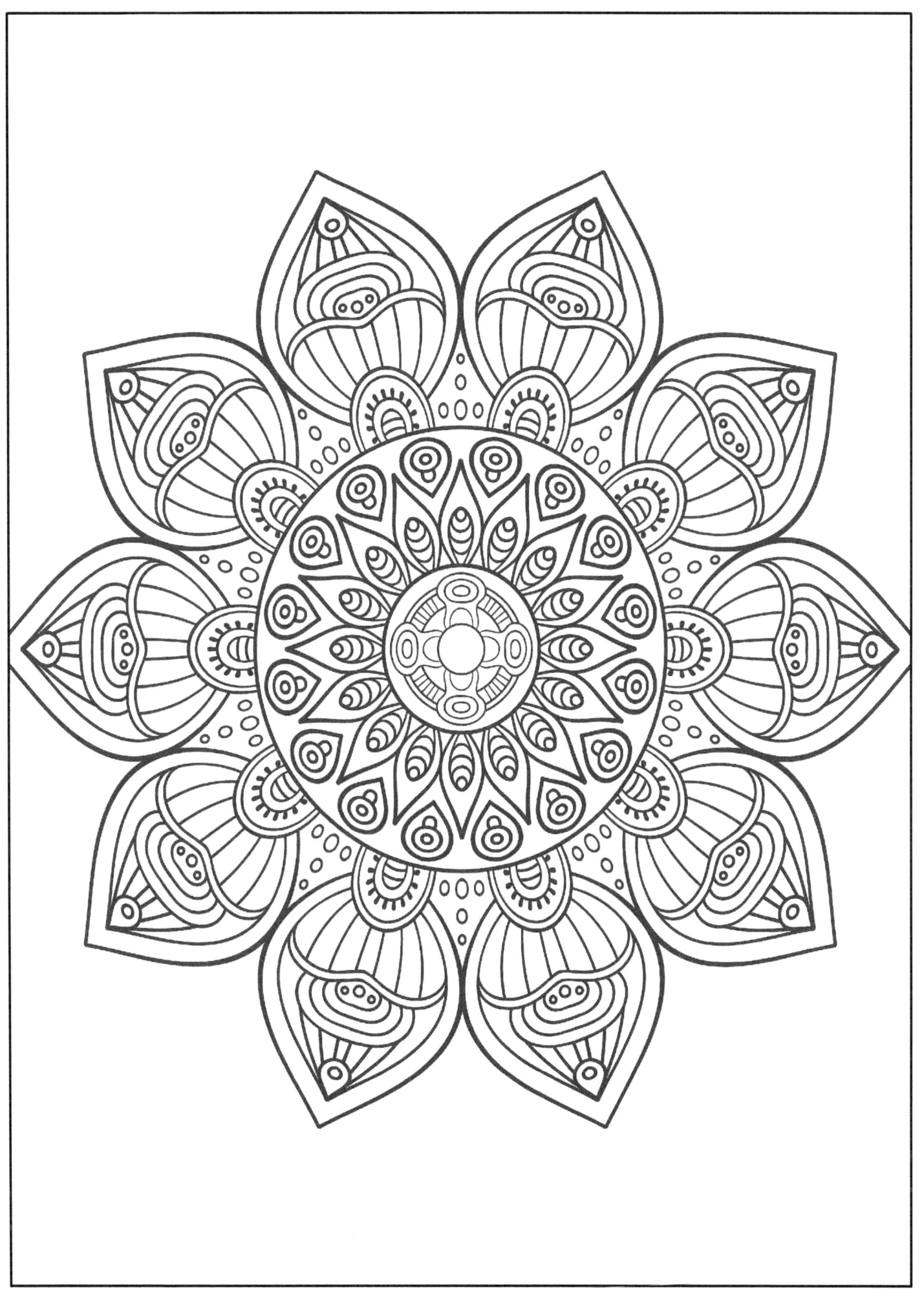

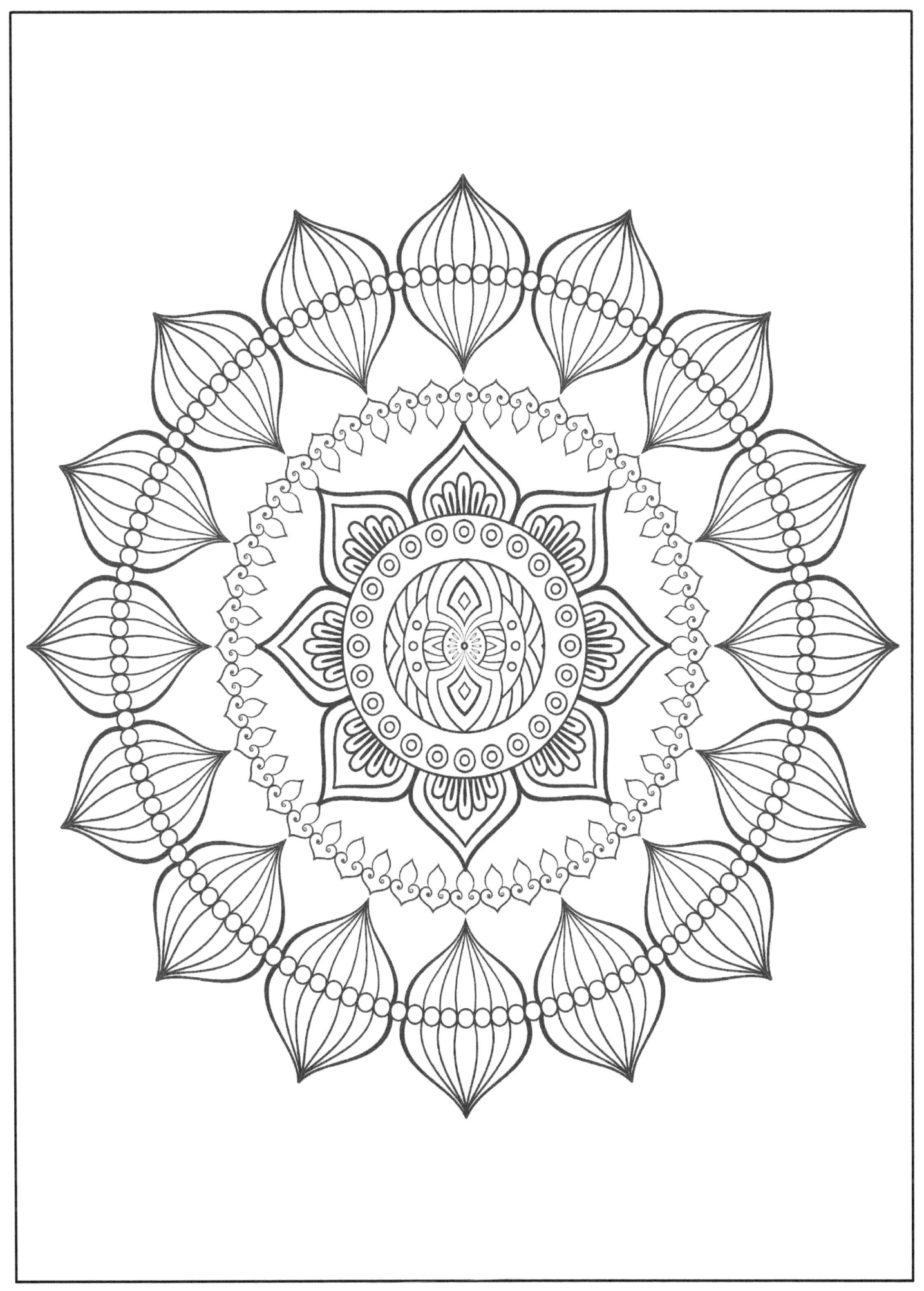

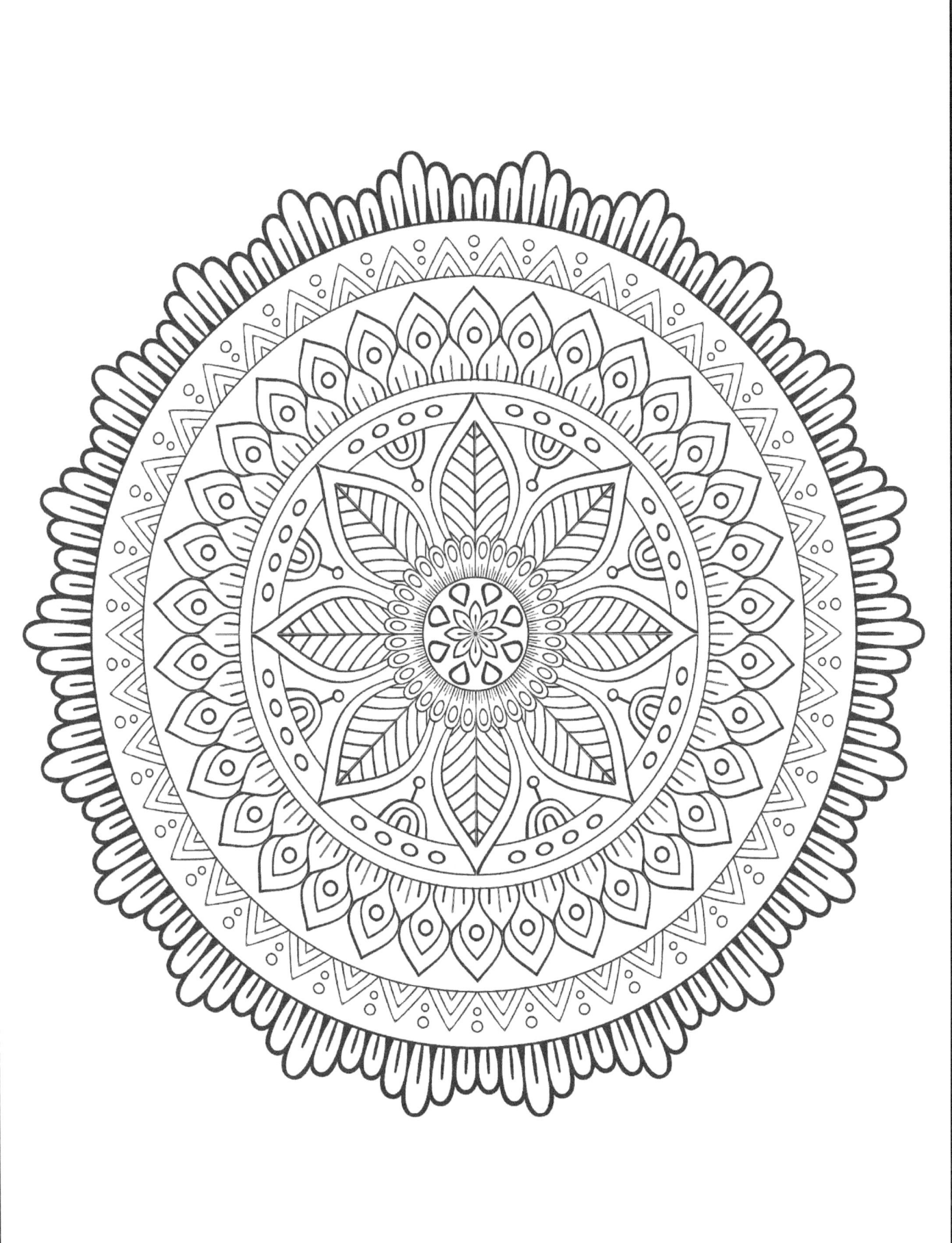

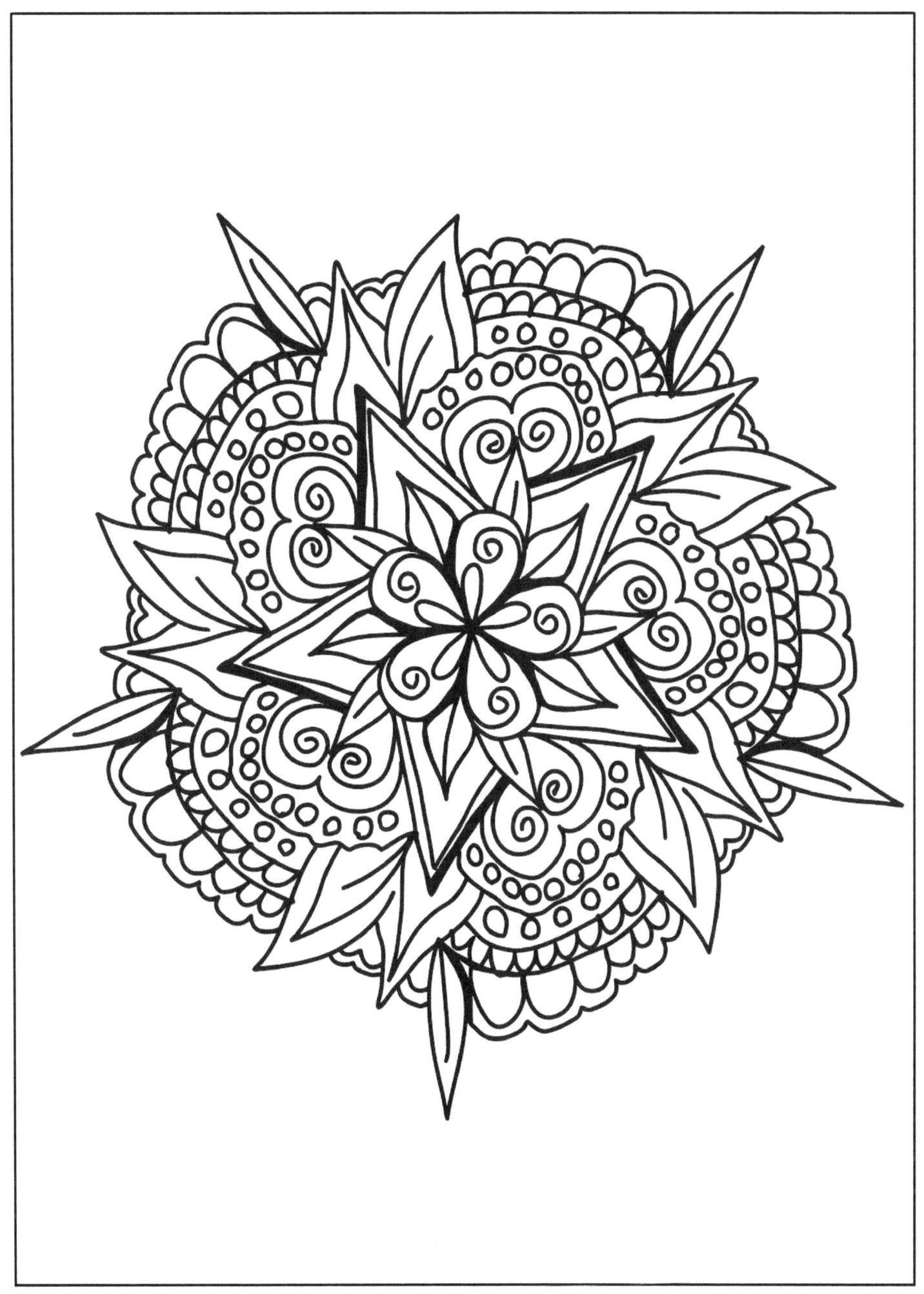

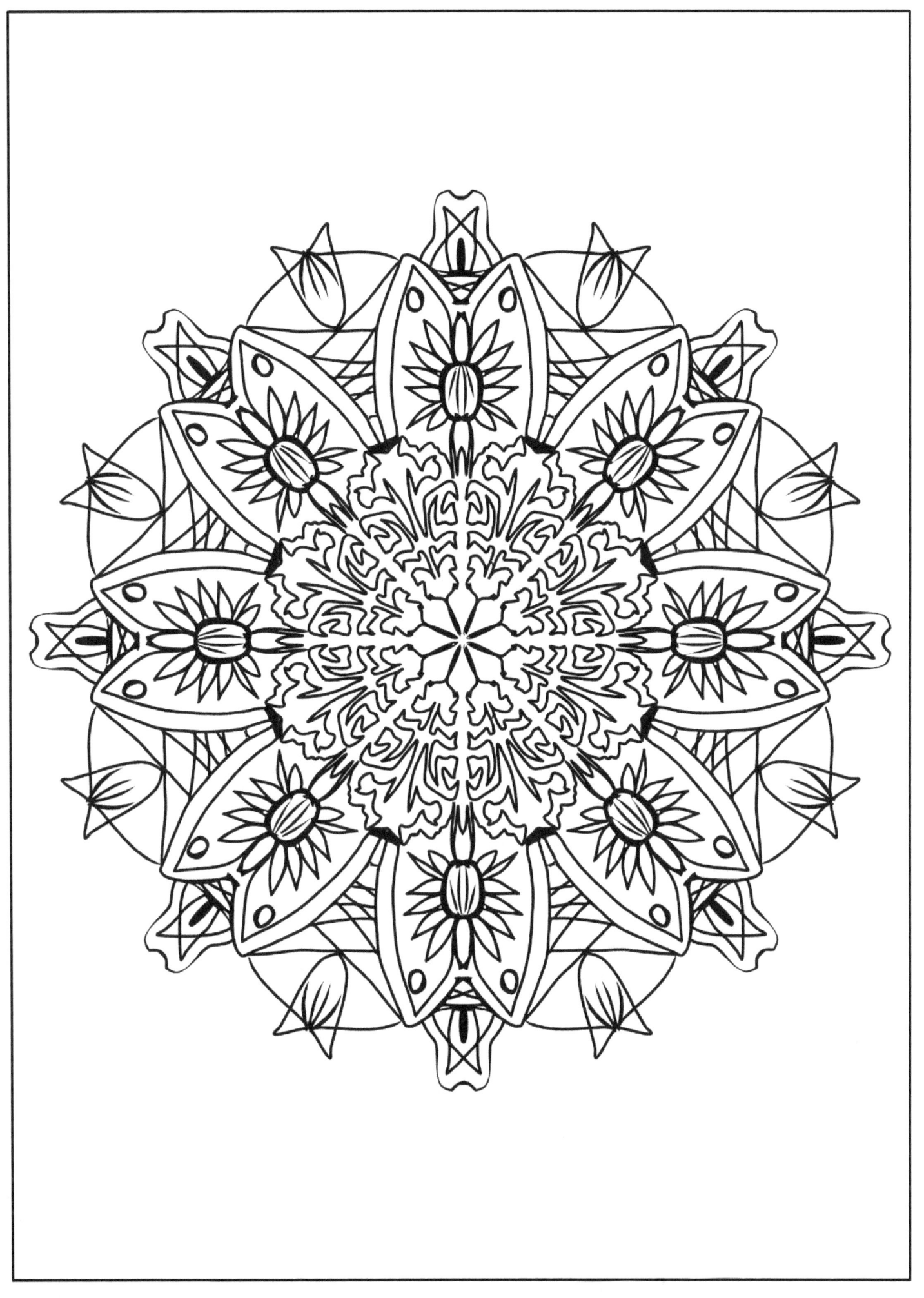

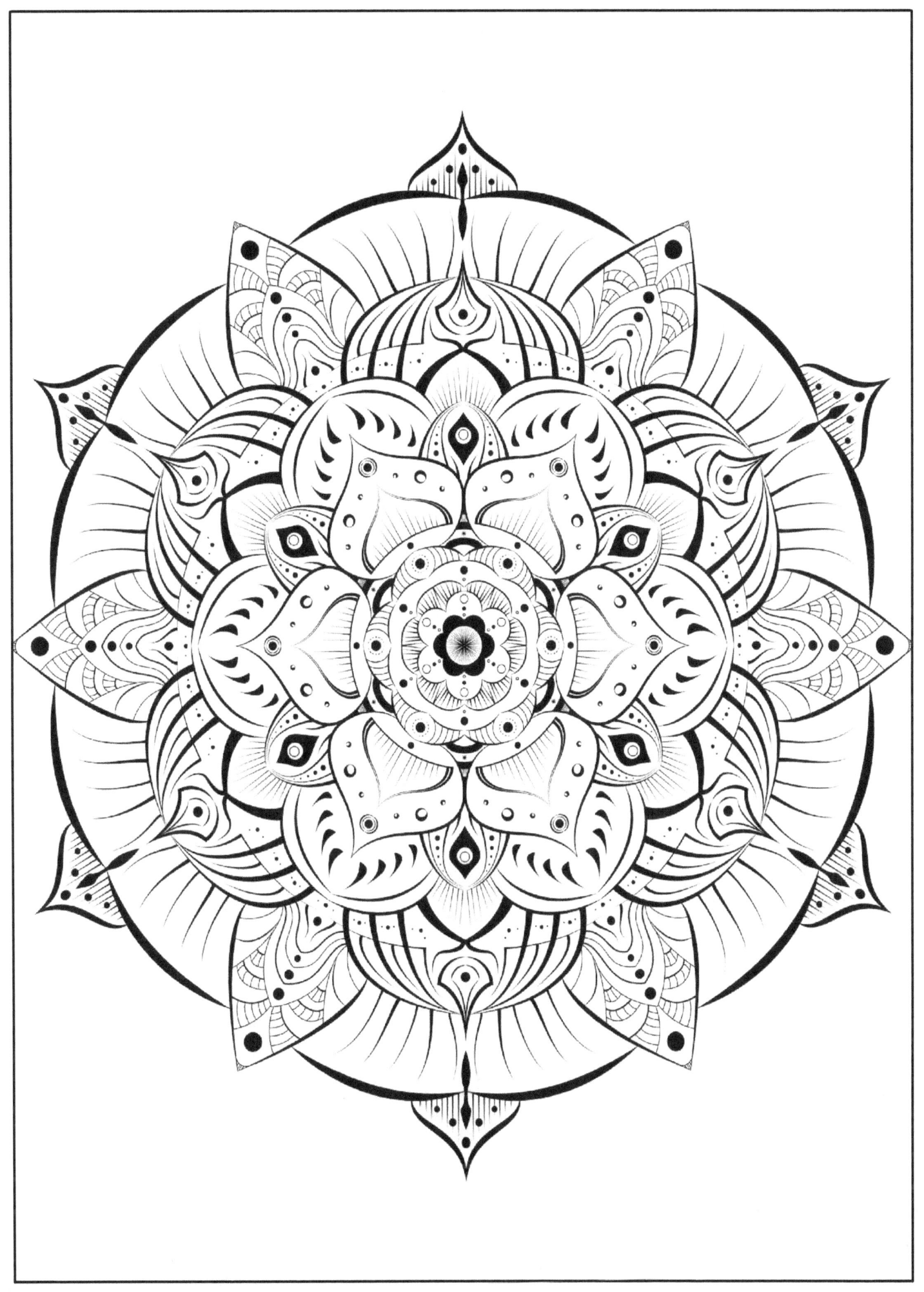

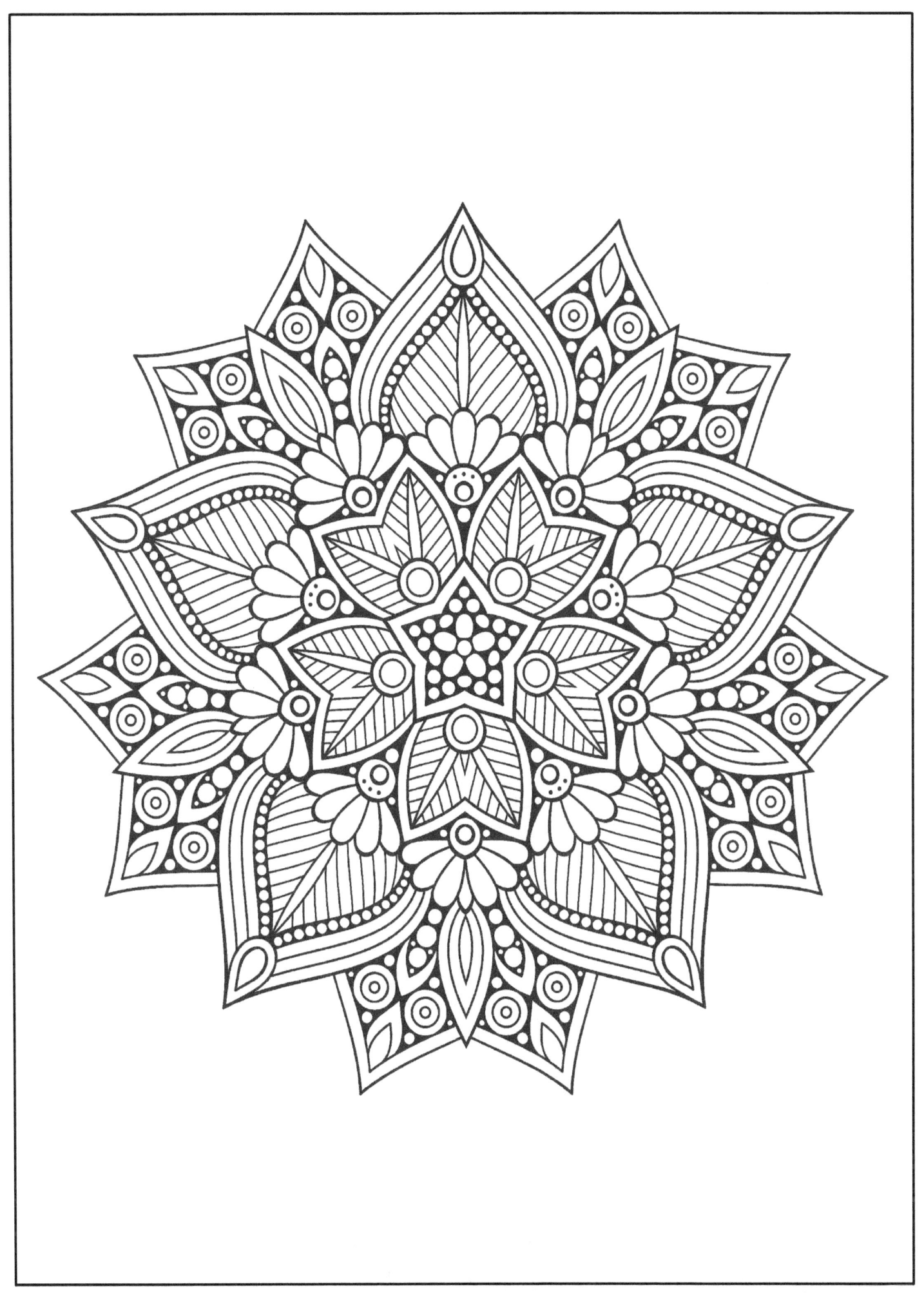

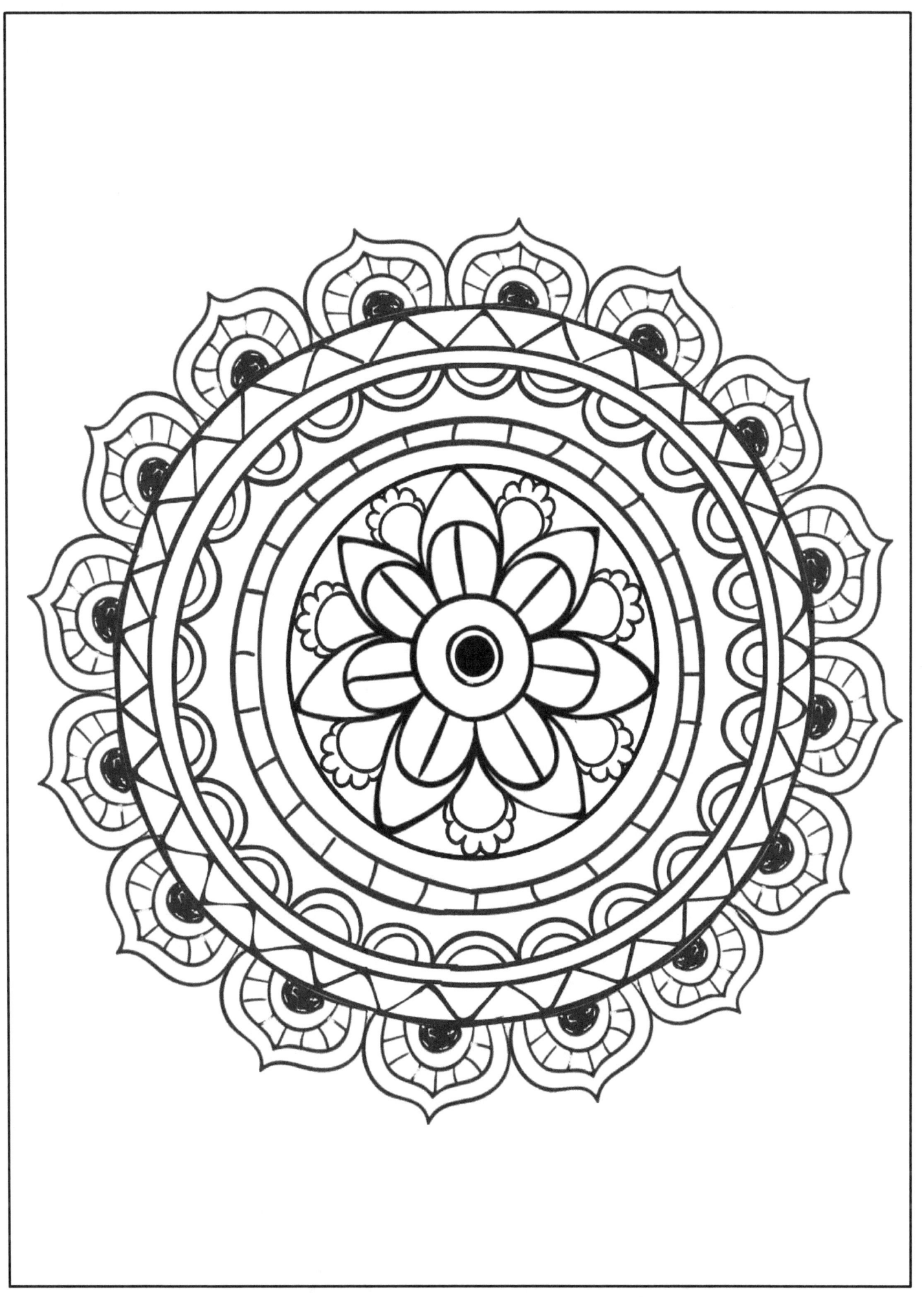

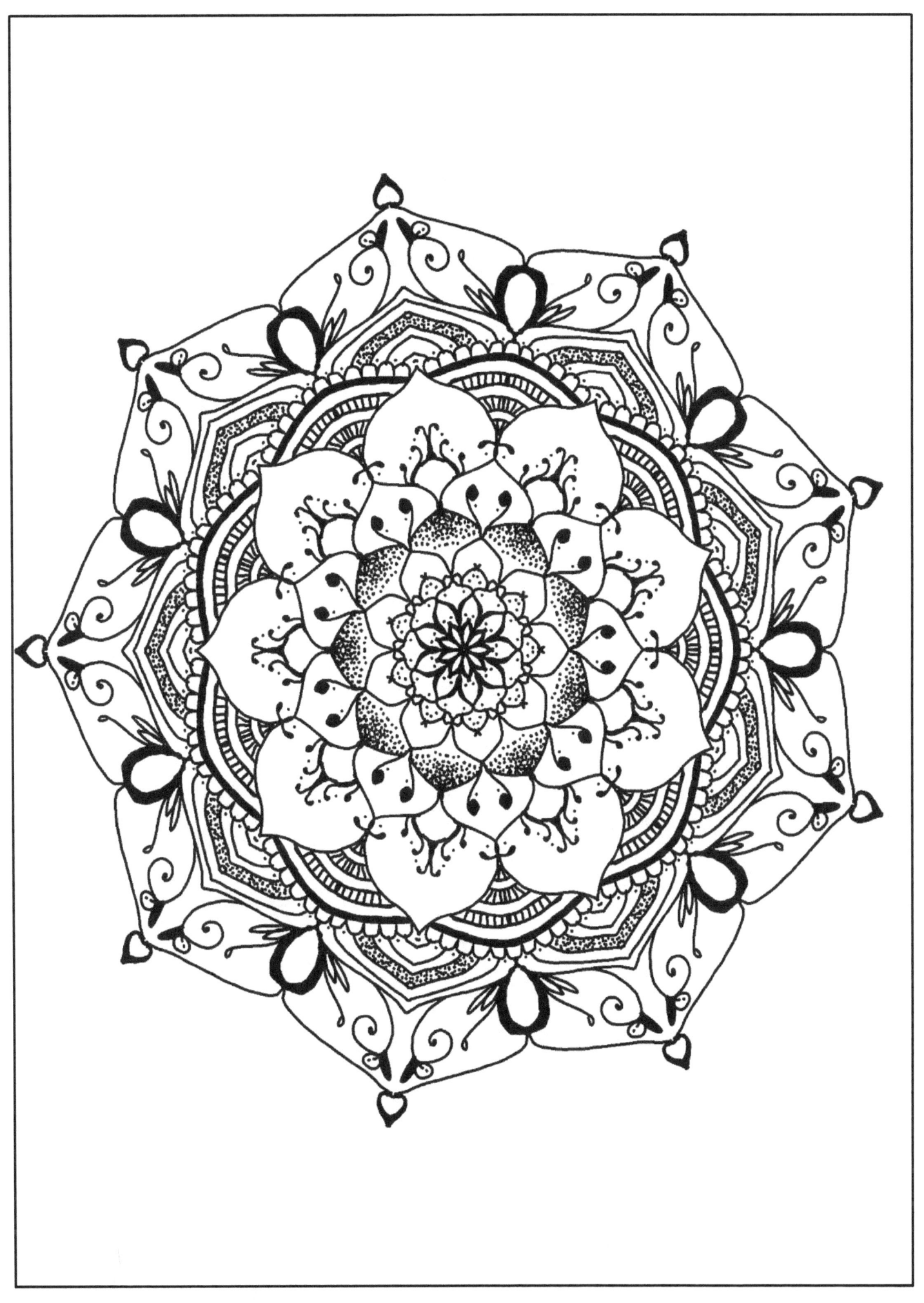

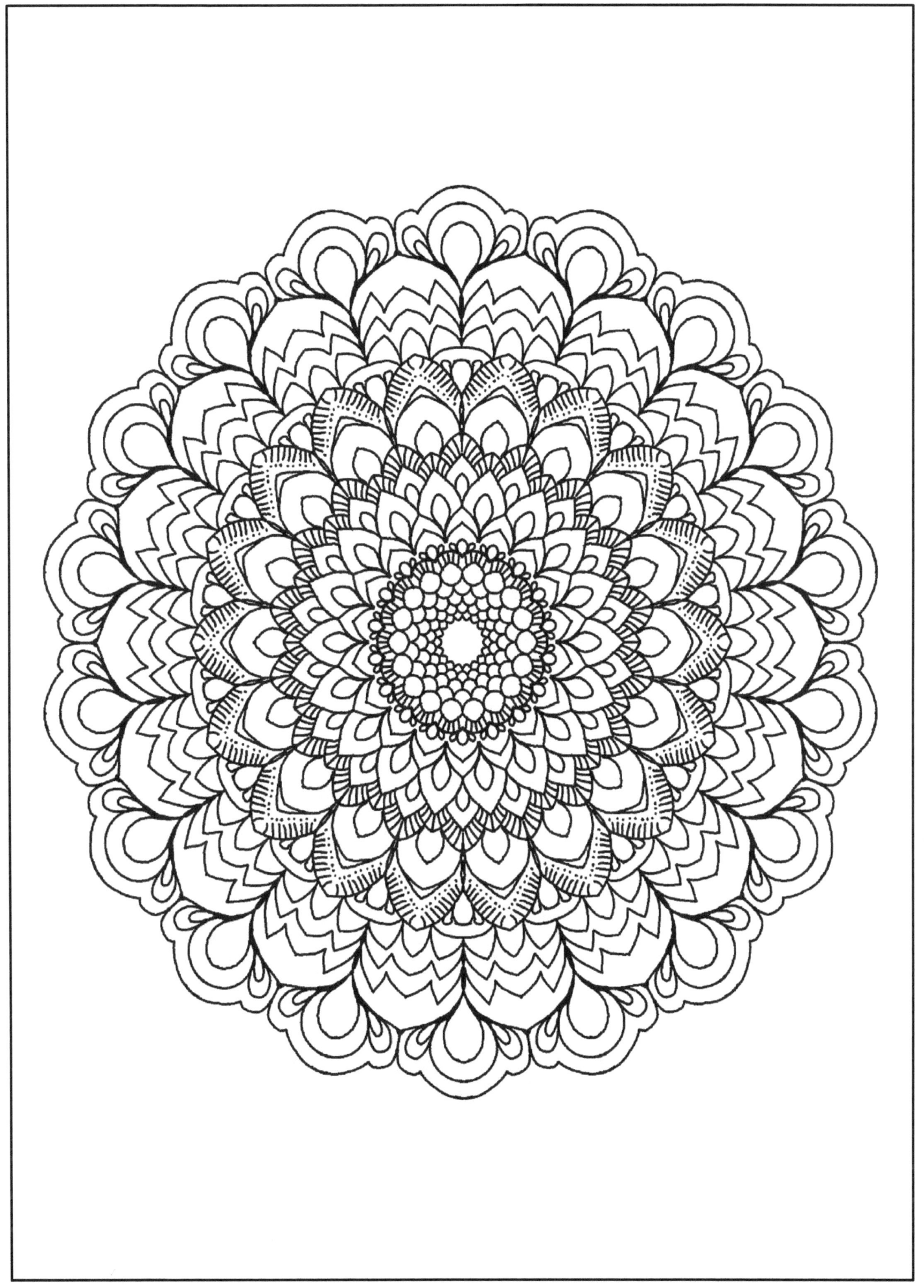

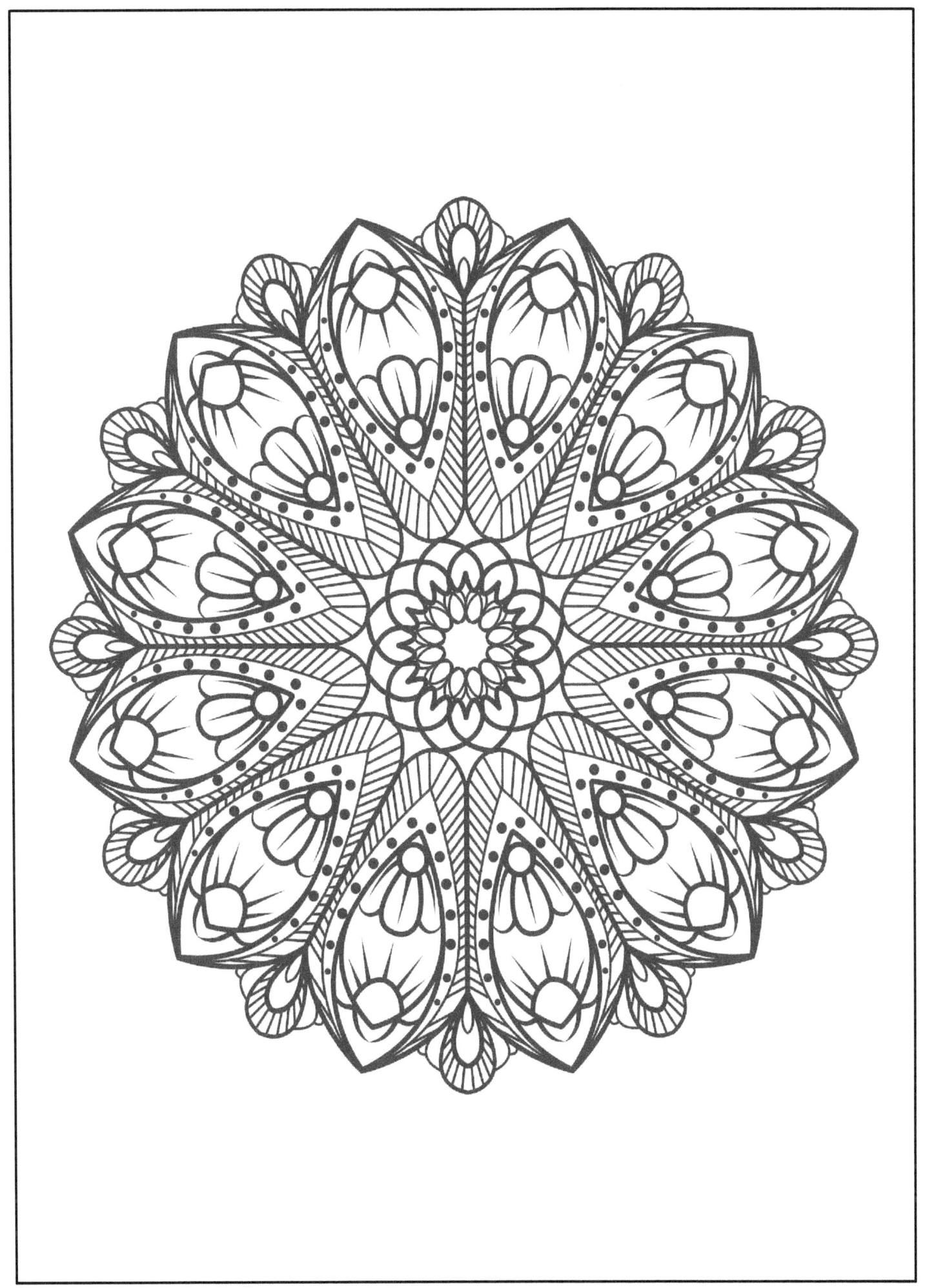

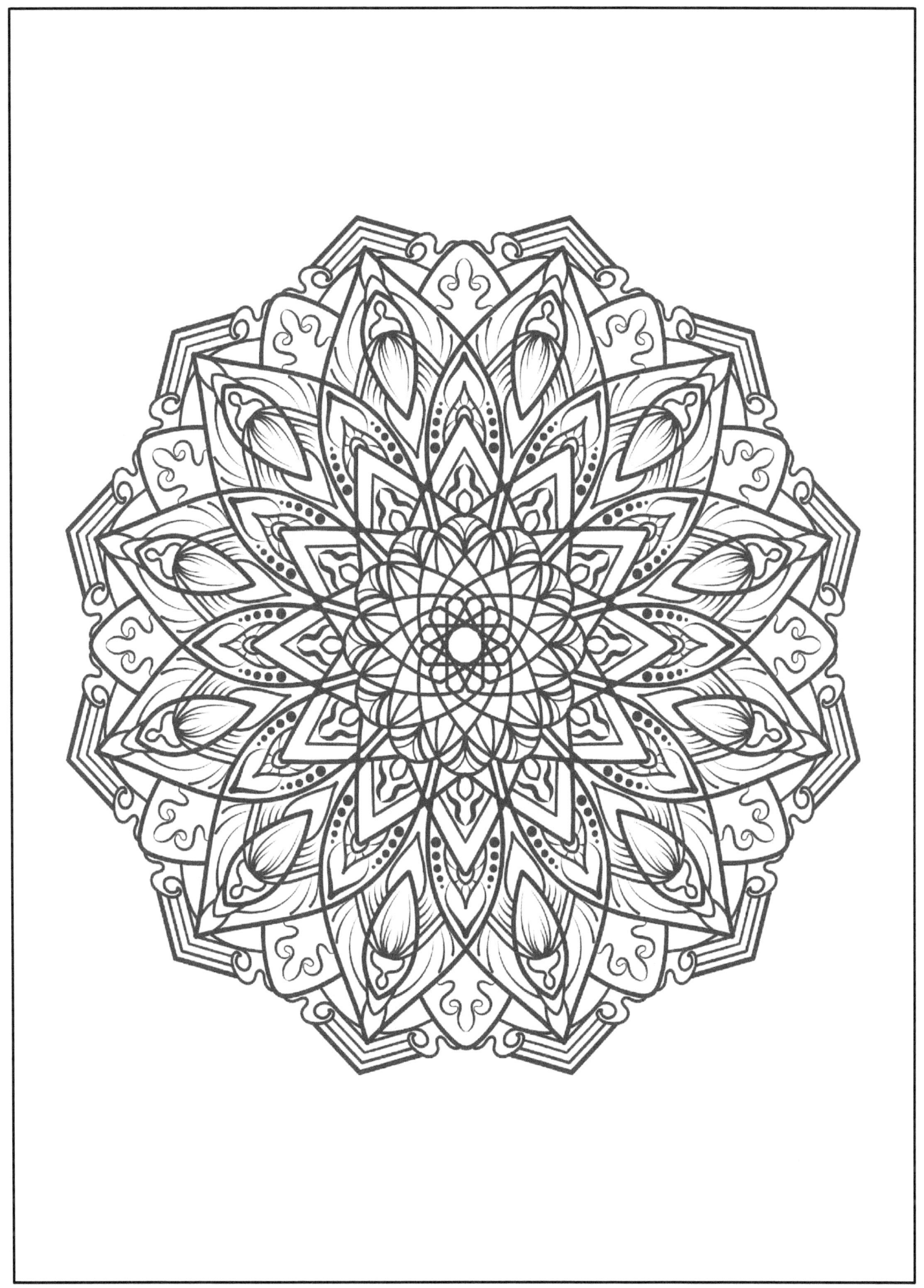

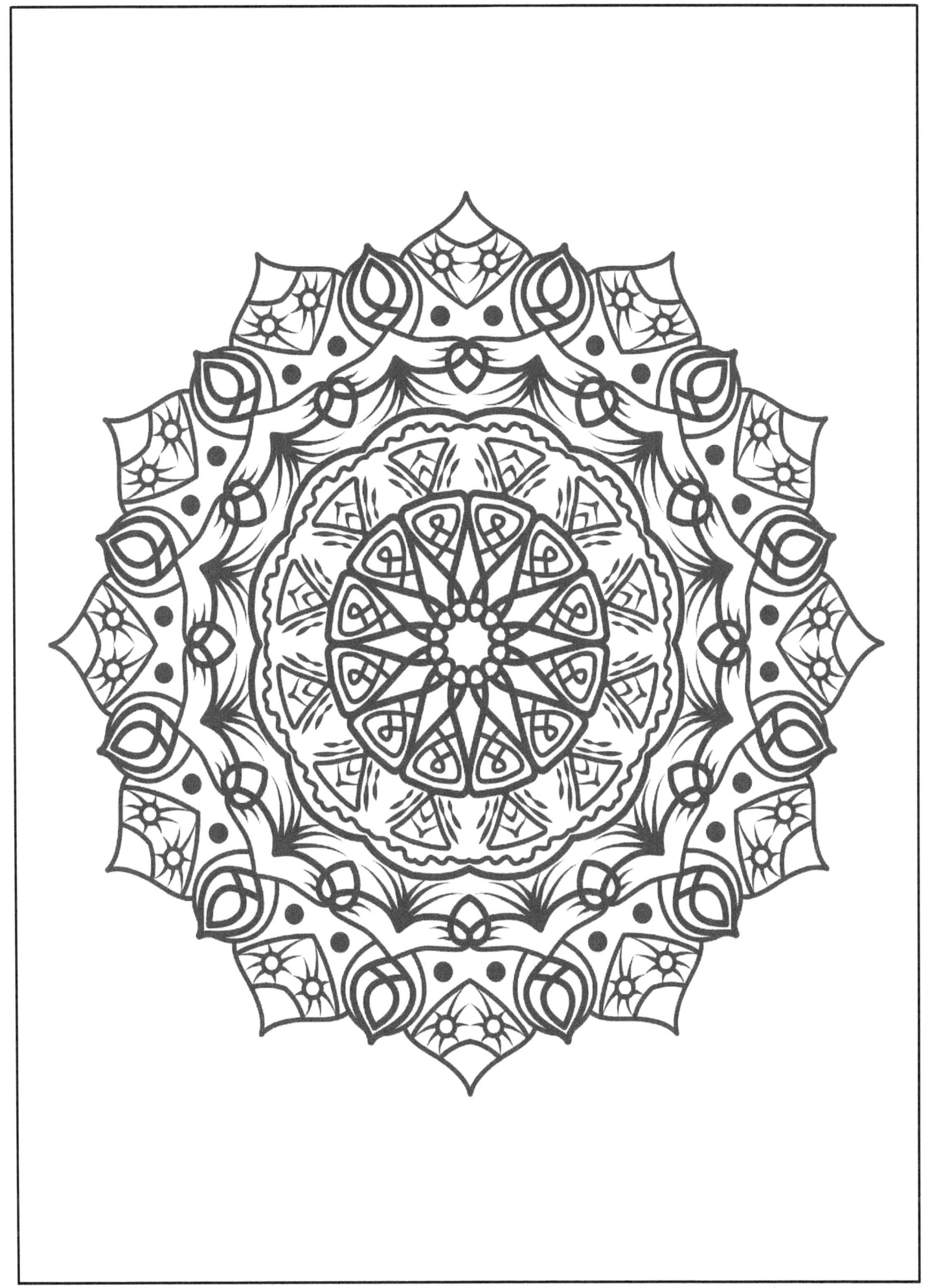

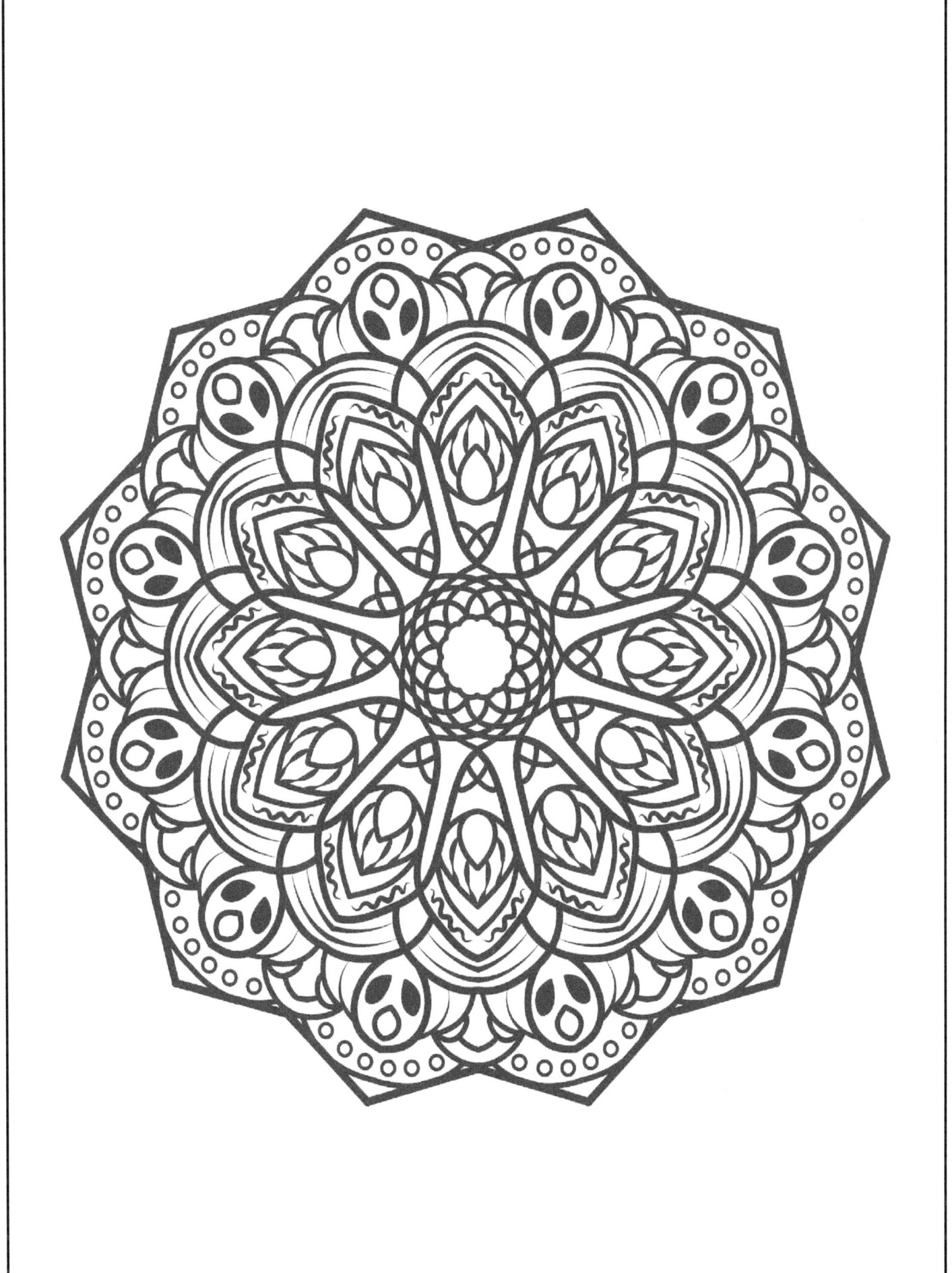

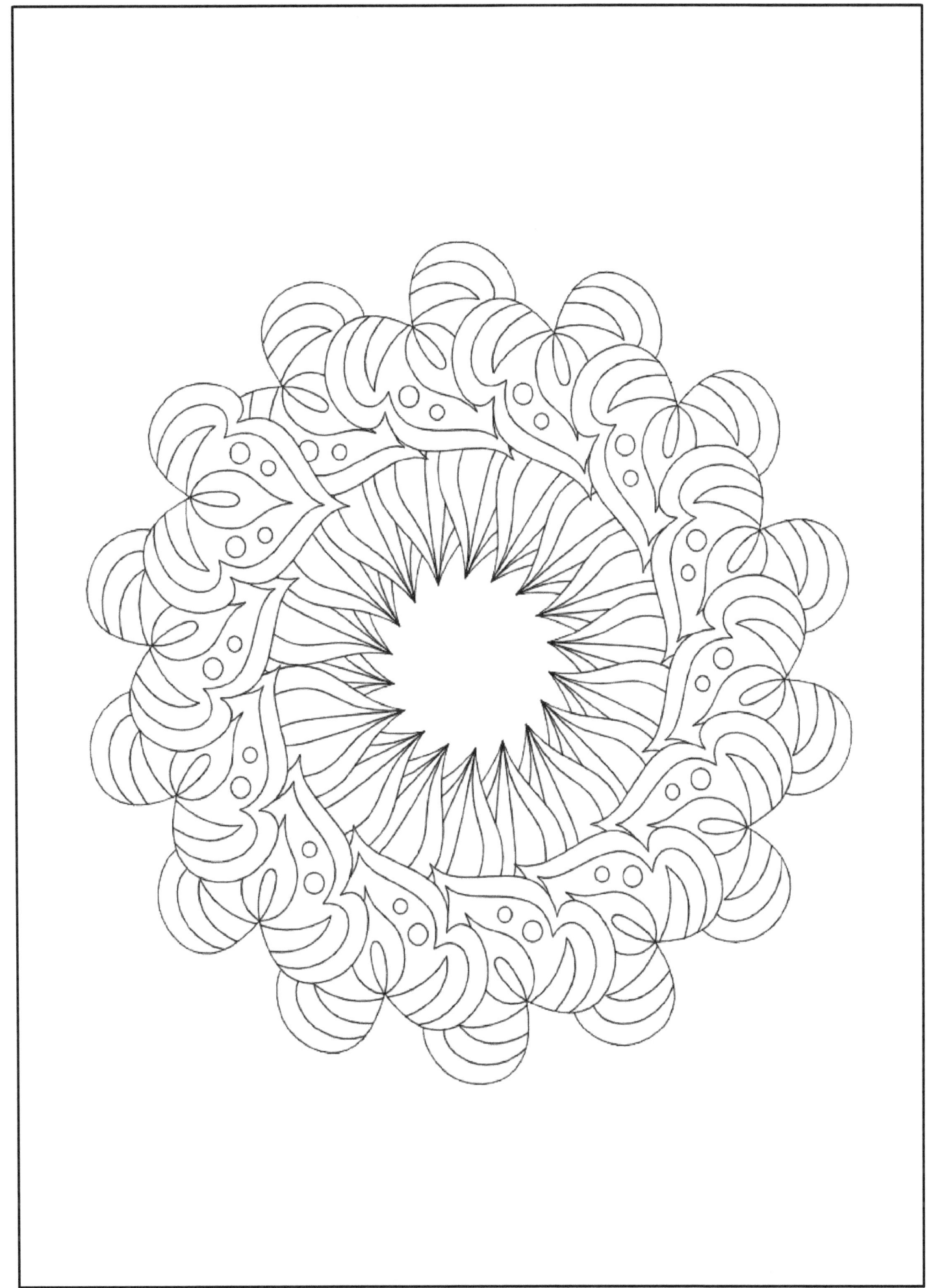

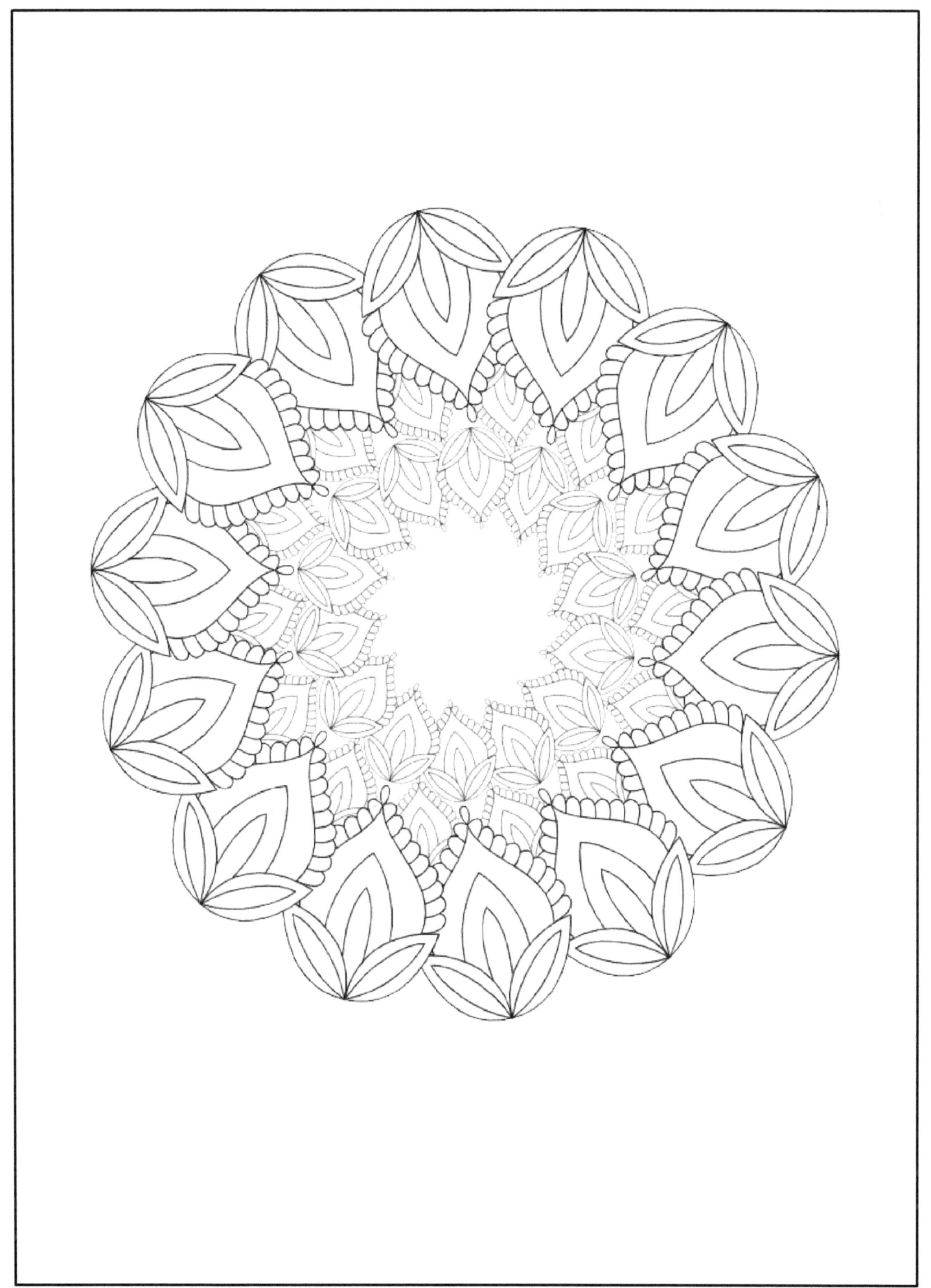

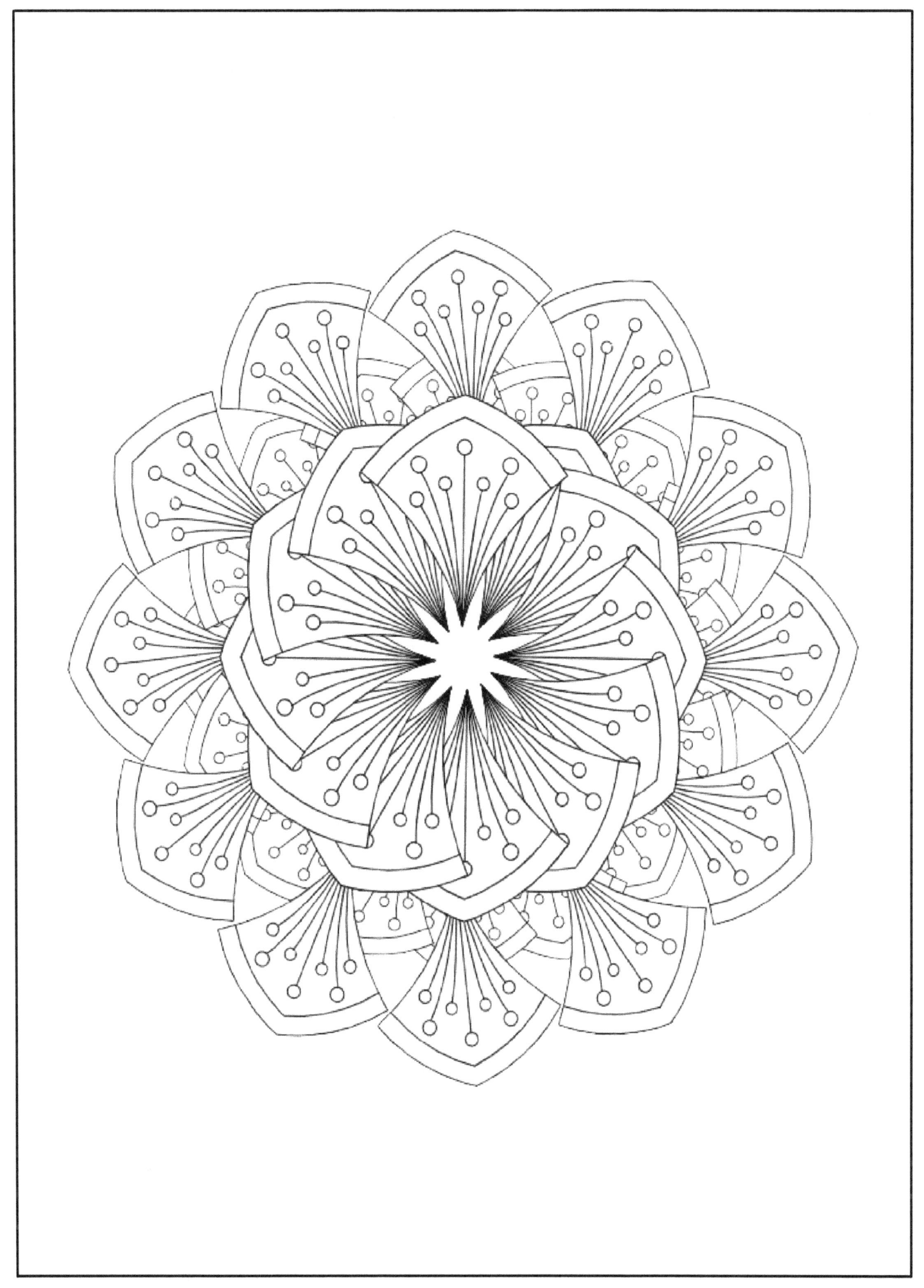

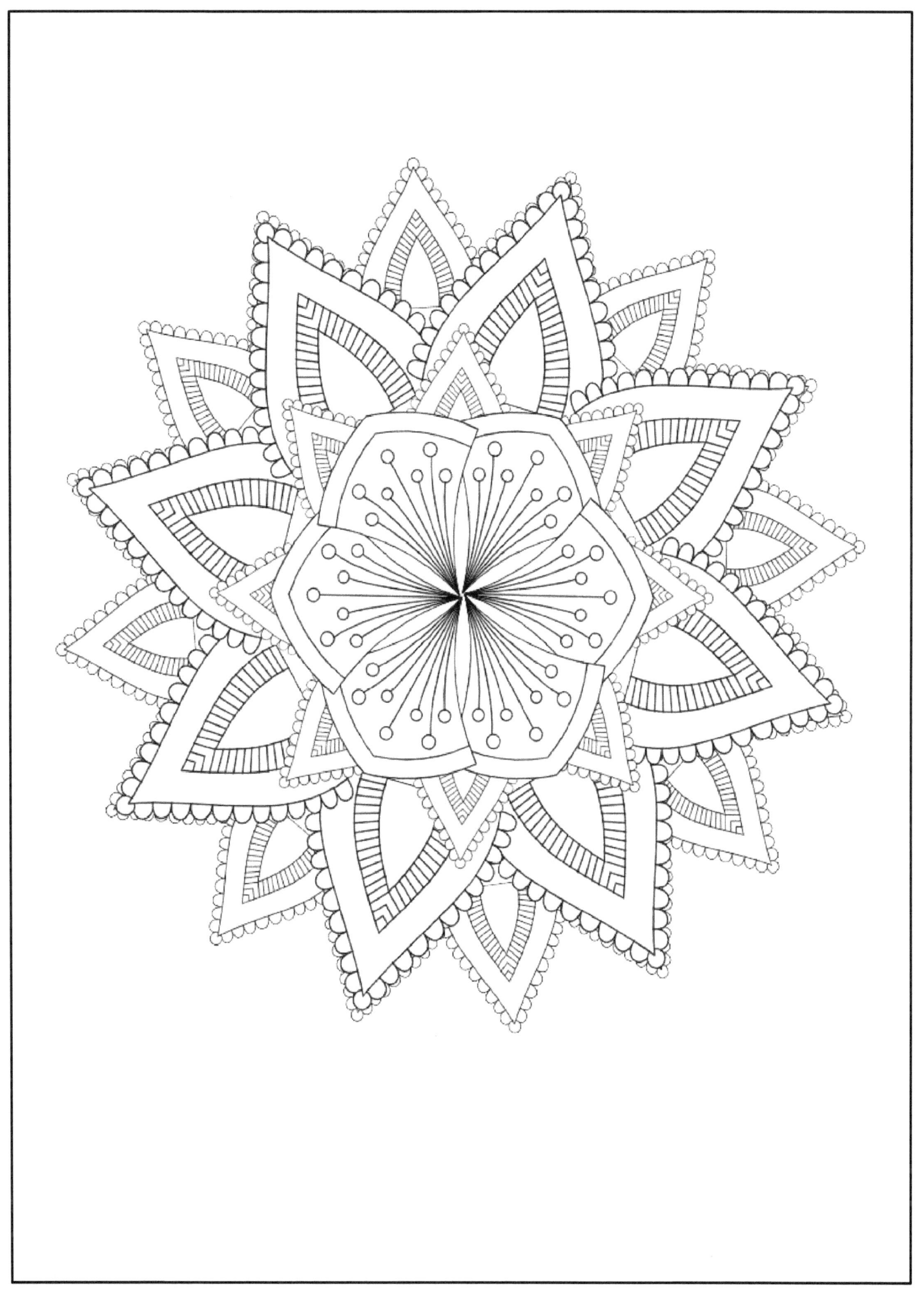

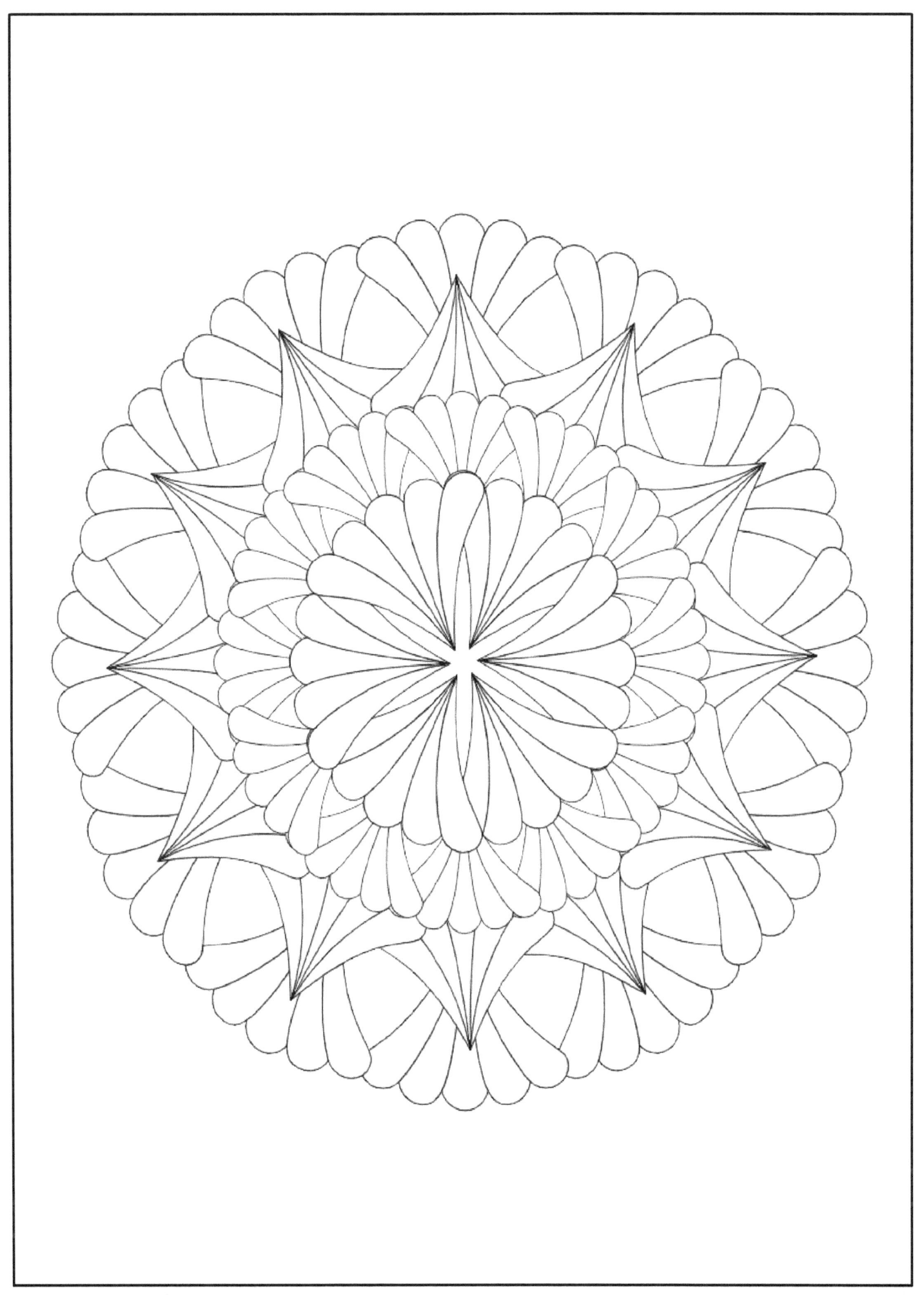

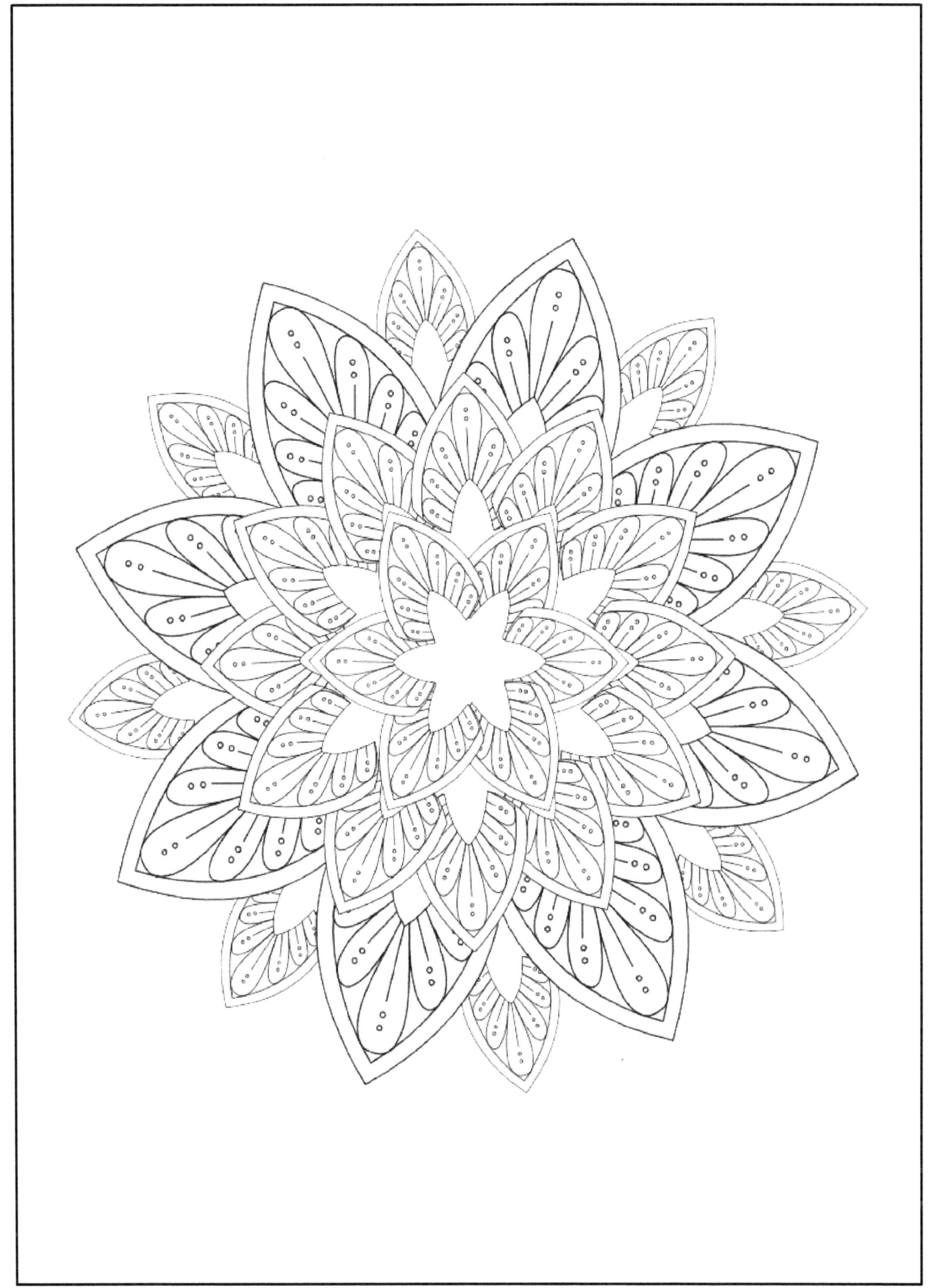

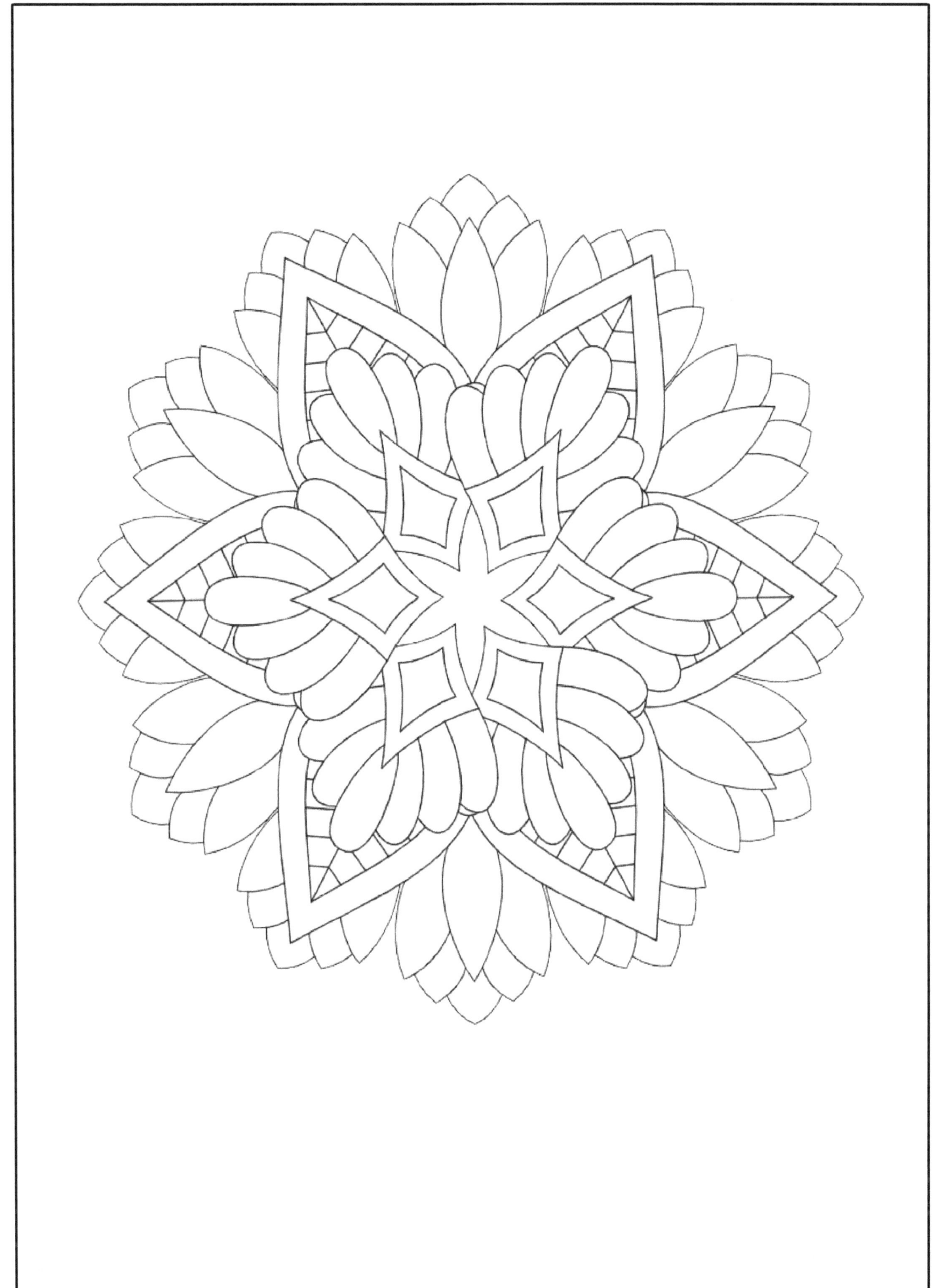

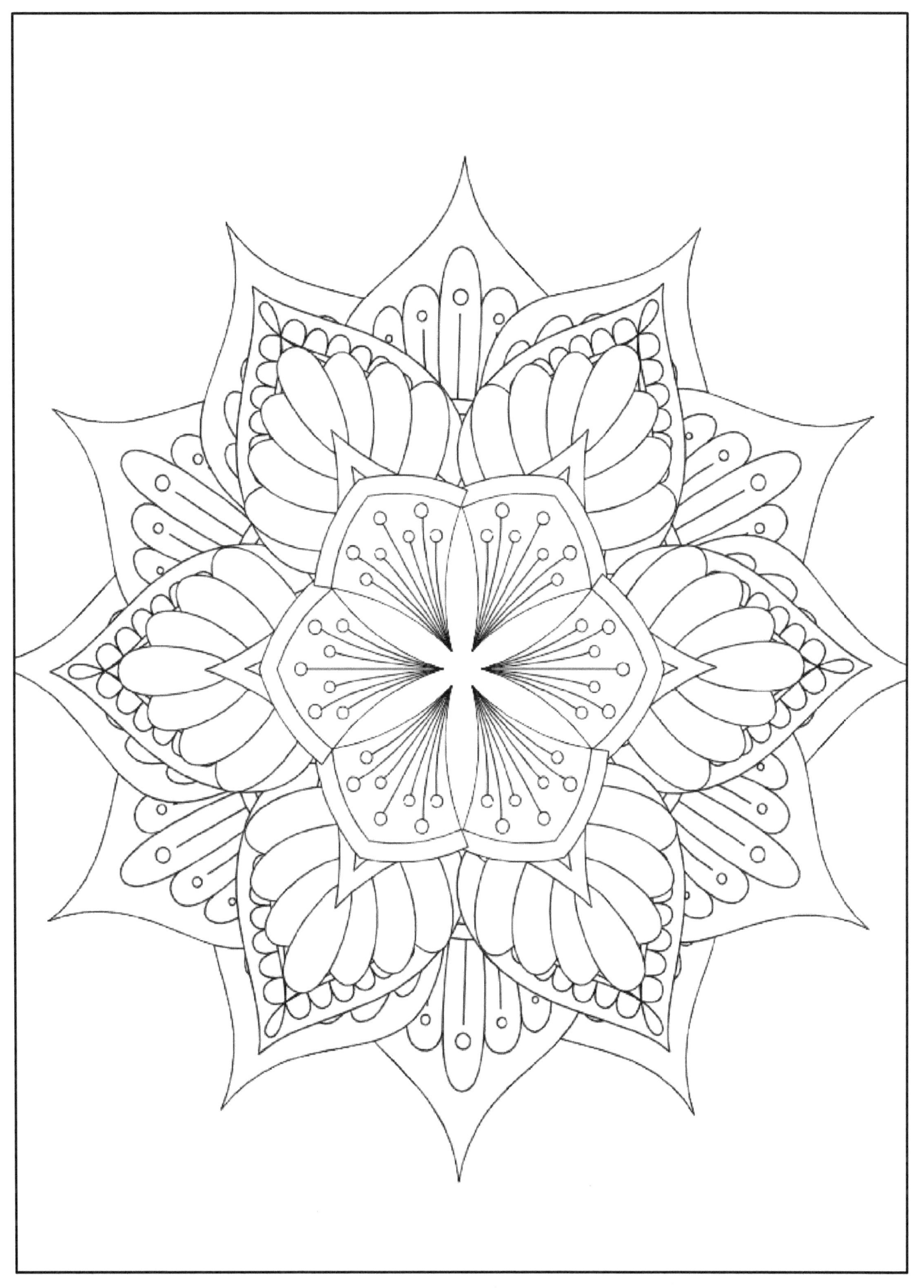

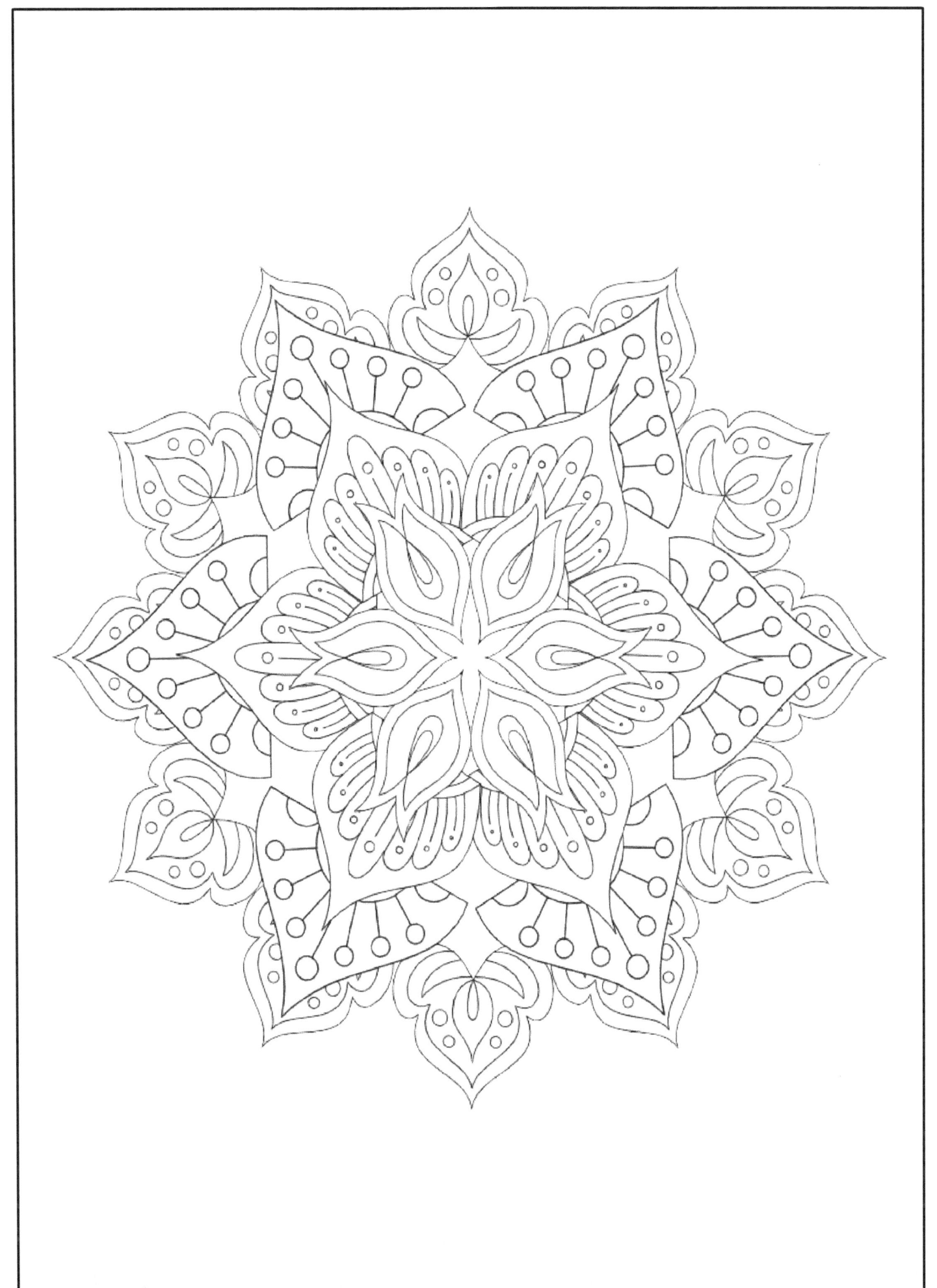

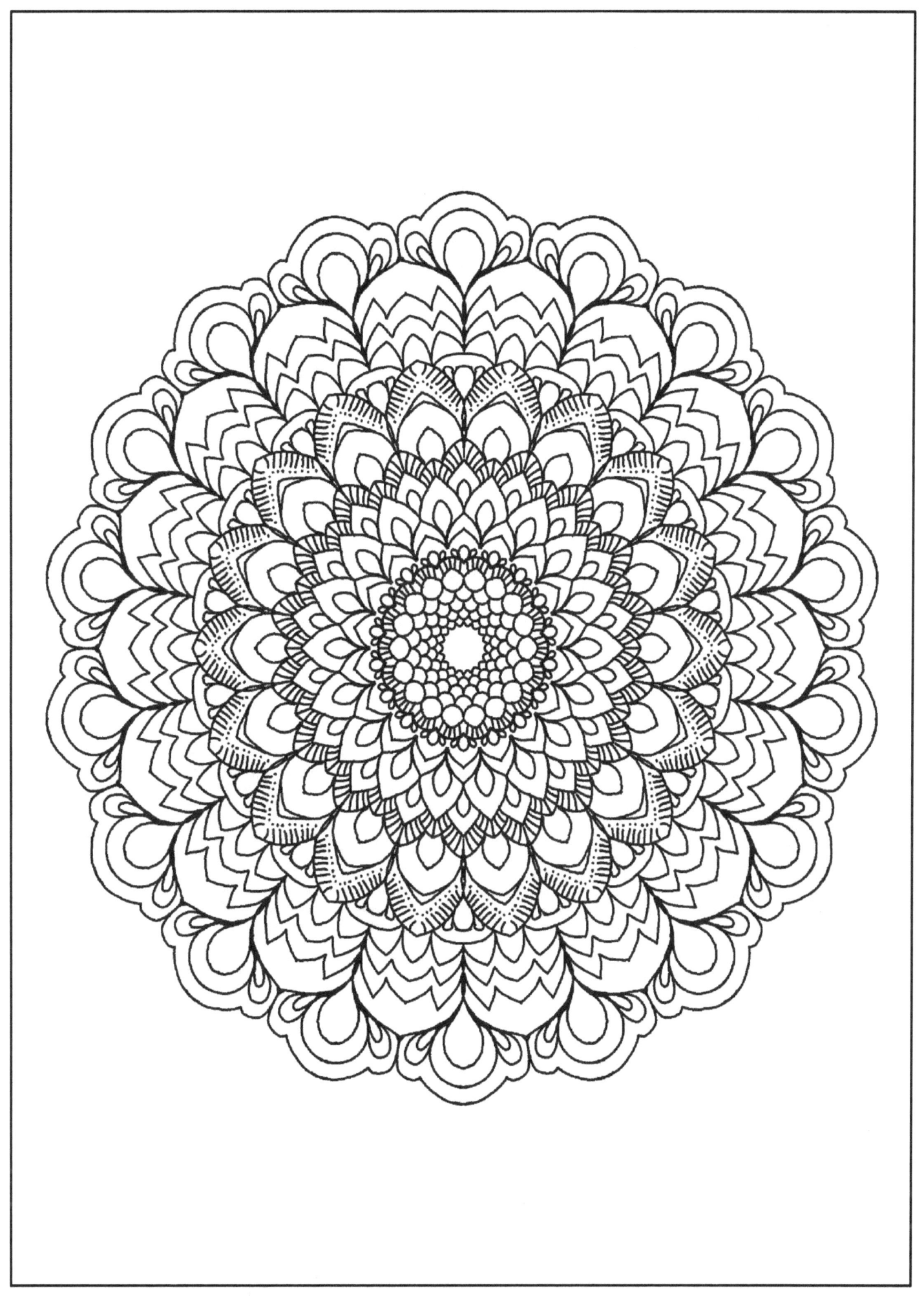

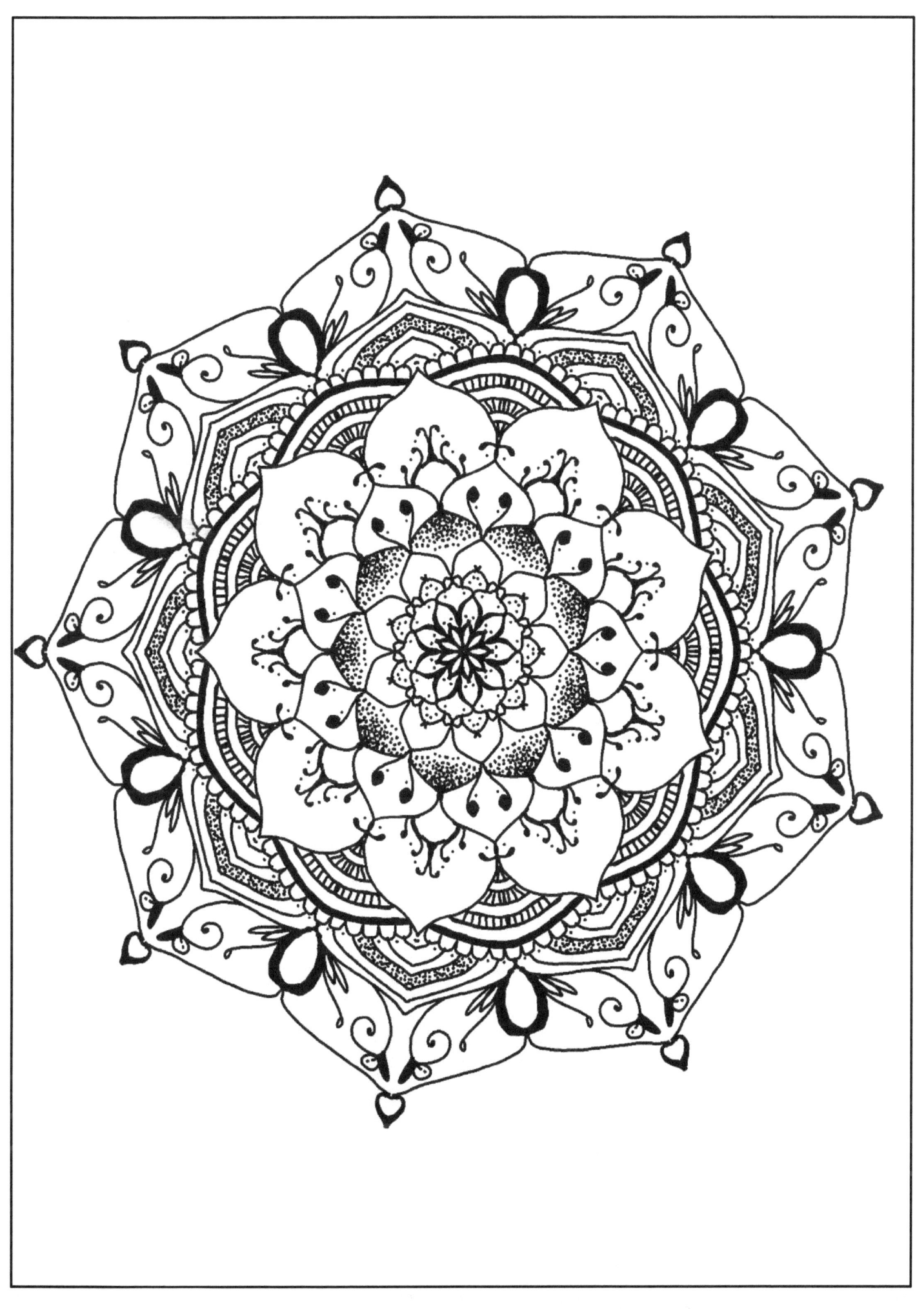